STRATEGIES FOR HELPING VICTIMS
OF ELDER MISTREATMENT

SAGE HUMAN SERVICES GUIDES, VOLUME 53

SAGE HUMAN SERVICES GUIDES

a series of books edited by ARMAND LAUFFER and CHARLES D. GARVIN. Published in cooperation with the University of Michigan School of Social Work and other organizations.

A **SAGE** HUMAN SERVICES GUIDE **53**

STRATEGIES FOR HELPING VICTIMS OF ELDER MISTREATMENT

Risa S. BRECKMAN
Ronald D. ADELMAN

Published in cooperation with the University of Michigan School of Social Work

SAGE PUBLICATIONS
The Publishers of Professional Social Science
Newbury Park   Beverly Hills   London   New Delhi

In memory of
Howard Segars,
mentor, colleague, and friend,
whose compassion, commitment, and vision continue to guide us.

For information address:

SAGE Publications, Inc.
2111 West Hillcrest Drive
Newbury Park, California 91320

SAGE Publications Inc.
275 South Beverly Drive
Beverly Hills
California 90212

SAGE Publications Ltd.
28 Banner Street
London EC1Y 8QE
England

SAGE PUBLICATIONS India Pvt. Ltd.
M-32 Market
Greater Kailash I
New Delhi 110 048 India

Printed in the United States of America

Library of Congress Cataloging-in-Publication Data

Breckman, Risa S.
    Strategies for helping victims of elder abuse.

    (Sage human services guides ; v. 53)
    Bibliography: p.
    1. Abused aged—Services for—United States.
2. Social work with the aged—United States.
I. Adelman, Ronald D.   II. Title.   III. Series.
HV1461.B74   1988   362.6   88-11352
ISBN 0-8039-3094-1 (pbk.)

FIRST PRINTING 1988

CONTENTS

PREFACE

Violence has become part of our daily lives: We read about it in the newspapers, see it on television, experience it on the streets of our cities and towns. And for all the times we are aware of it, there are many more times that violence occurs without our knowledge. Behind closed doors of more American homes than we would care to admit, parents abuse children, husbands abuse wives, and elderly people are abused and neglected by spouses, caregivers, children, and other family members. It is hard to imagine that old age, respected and revered in some societies, could be so exploited and mistreated in our own. Yet the statistics tell us that it is so. An estimated one million older people are abused and neglected each year in the United States. But this problem has emerged only recently as a significant social issue that deserves to be thoroughly researched as well as addressed on a practical level. In order to help these victims, professionals need to be educated about this shocking phenomenon.

With this thought-provoking book, Risa Breckman and Ronald Adelman provide a valuable guide for students who are beginning their exploration of this disturbing topic, as well as for physicians, social workers, clergy, nurses, and other professionals who work with older people. Comprehensive theoretical and "how-to" information on detection, assessment, and intervention are thoroughly covered within the context of geriatric practice—an interdisciplinary collaboration among medical, nursing, legal, and social work professionals.

Those of us working with older people need to get involved with the issue of elder abuse and neglect in two ways. The first step is to understand the problem and develop detection, intervention, and prevention strategies so that we can help elderly victims today. The second, broader step is to examine the underlying societal attitudes and institutional policies that set the stage for the mistreatment of the older population, so that we may be able actively to participate in helping to reduce the incidence and prevalence of elder abuse and neglect. For as the number of older people increases in the United States, so may cases of mistreatment. We, as professionals, are extremely fortunate to have this groundbreaking book to help us deal with this critical problem, as well as to lay the foundation for future research and policies.

—Robert N. Butler, M.D.
March 8, 1988

ACKNOWLEDGMENTS

Many of our colleagues, friends, and family have been tremendously helpful to us in this endeavor. We wish to thank Karl Pillemer for his apt criticisms, delivered always with humor and support, and for his written contribution to the manuscript; Flora Colao, whose compassionate teaching about the needs of victims has inspired and informed our work; Pam Ansell, Andrea Nevins, and Alice Vachss for helping us create an accurate, readable, and practical text; Judith Adelson, Marcia Gitomer, and Peter Wolk for providing encouragement and support when we thought we would never finish; Terry Hendrix for his patience and enthusiasm for our work; Jane Auch, Joel Brauser, and Alan Ross for timely and careful editing; Olivia Harris for helping to type the manuscript; Robert N. Butler and Lucy Friedman for taking risks with and being enthusiastic about new and creative elder abuse programs; the contributing authors in Chapters 4 and 5 for enhancing the scope of this book; and to the victims who freely shared with us a difficult part of their lives in order to help others.

INTRODUCTION

Strategies for Helping Victims of Elder Mistreatment was written to provide social service, legal, and health care professionals with a practical guide for dealing with a difficult and alarming social phenomenon. The intentional physical, financial, and psychological abuse and neglect of individuals 60 years of age and older, by family members is an issue that we have been studying on a daily basis for over five years. This book reflects knowledge gained from our direct work with victims, our training of thousands of professionals and students in assisting victims, our program development experience, and our case consultation work with professionals. Our intention is to provide students and professionals interested in gerontology and domestic violence with some practical guidelines, insights, and strategies for detecting, assessing, and intervening with competent elderly victims of family mistreatment.

A theoretical framework for understanding the phenomenon of elder mistreatment is provided in Chapters 1 and 2. Chapter 1 defines elder mistreatment, discusses its incidence and the characteristics of the victims and perpetrators, and examines risk factors of elder mistreatment. Chapter 2 explores the relationship between gerontological and family violence knowledge and elder mistreatment. Chapter 3 provides an extensive review of the signs and symptoms of mistreatment, and factors mitigating against its detection are explored. In Chapter 4 a framework for assessing mistreatment cases is provided and, using this model as a guide, Chapter 5 discusses intervention strategies. In Chapter 6, six professionals respond to case studies. These contributing authors, representing the fields of law, medicine, nursing, and social work, discuss their respective professional roles in helping victims achieve a life without violence. Chapter 7 provides direct testimonies from victims of mistreatment. Each victim discusses her own victimization and healing process, proving victims can and do overcome abusive circumstances. Chapter 8 concludes the book with suggestions on future directions in the areas of research, training, and program development. Many elements of the book can also be extrapolated for use as materials for training professionals on the detection, assessment, and intervention with victims.

The authors hope that this book will prove useful to you in your work with victims of elder mistreatment, and that through your work fewer older people will suffer from this problem.

Chapter 1

ELDER MISTREATMENT DEFINED

Lack of uniformity and agreement by researchers, policy analysts, and practitioners in the definition of elder mistreatment is a problem that has plagued research in this field. As a result, comparing and analyzing research findings is difficult and progress in understanding this form of domestic mistreatment has been impeded. In this chapter, we will explore various definitions of elder mistreatment and will define the terms used throughout this volume. Recent research findings on incidence and prevalence of elder mistreatment and a summary of current information regarding the profile of the victims and the abusers will also be presented, as will causes and risk factors. (The word "abuser" is used throughout this volume to mean "abuser and/or neglector.")

DEFINITIONS AND CONTROVERSIES

The inconsistent use of terminology is common throughout the literature. The development of precise definitions of *elder abuse* and *neglect* will represent a major advance in utilizing research findings, enabling researchers and practitioners to build on each other's work in order to provide a more solid information base.

The following will provide a framework from which we will derive a "working definition" of the terms and issues used throughout this book.

MISTREATMENT

Sociologist Tanya Johnson (1986, pp. 167-196) confronts the problem of definition by devising a framework to incorporate all circumstances that constitute "elder mistreatment." Johnson stresses the need for developing an intrinsic definition or conceptualization of the phenomenon and points out the redundancy of using the word *abuse* to define itself. When elder abuse is defined as "any abusive action inflicted by the abusers on adults 60 years of age or older," this hardly clarifies the matter. Johnson convincingly argues that it makes more sense to call the phenomenon of elder abuse and neglect "elder mistreatment."

Johnson proposes a four-stage definition: (1) the creation of an intrinsic definition, (2) the development of an extrinsic definition that specifies behavioral manifestations, (3) the formulation of an extrinsic definition that is able to measure the frequency, severity, and density of events, and (4) the assessment of the underlying causes of the mistreatment. The four stages will be examined in greater detail.

Intrinsic definition. Johnson's intrinsic definition of elder mistreatment is conceptualized as "self- or other inflicted suffering unnecessary to the maintenance of the quality of life of the older person." Although little work has been done concerning the etiology and prevalence of self-inflicted elder mistreatment, Johnson's definition fortunately is broad enough to encompass this. Suffering is defined as "intense and sustained pain and anguish." The intrinsic definition in this model attempts to differentiate normal, culturally acceptable mistreatment, such as yelling, from pathologic or abusive mistreatment, such as hitting. Johnson's intrinsic definition ultimately focuses on whether the older person has experienced pain and suffering to determine whether mistreatment has occurred. The intrinsic definition proposed is not site specific, so it includes, for example, institutional abuse as well as elder mistreatment occurring in the home.

Extrinsic definition. The extrinsic definition outlines specific behaviors that may be evidence of mistreatment under four categories: physical, psychological, sociological, and legal. Johnson states that "labelling the categories facilitates the identification process." Although the physical and psychological categories may be familiar, the latter two deserve further elaboration. Sociological mistreatment, as defined by Johnson, "represents suffering as a consequence of not being integrated into the primary group setting as a result of the elder's resistance or the coercion on the part of others." The behavioral manifestations included in the legal category include material exploitation, such as misuse of money; exploitation of person, such as denial of rights to self-determination of competent older people; and theft, manifested, for example, by extortion of property.

Intensity and density. This part of Johnson's definition assesses the frequency and severity (intensity) of the mistreatment, and measures the variety of forms of mistreatment in each individual case (density). By obtaining a clear sense of the degree of intensity and density, the worker can determine the extent of the intervention required and ascertain the urgency of intervention as well.

Cause and intent. The last part of Johnson's definition addresses the immediate cause of the mistreatment. The need to identify the intent of the act is stressed, as this knowledge will help determine the most appropriate approach to intervention. Without knowledge of intent, intervention strategies are severely hampered. If, for example, the neglect or abuse was unintentional, this knowledge may guide the worker to develop an approach with a major emphasis on education. However, if the mistreatment was deliberate, a different approach would be indicated. This causal definition is also included because it allows for the development of protective measures for the victim.

Although Johnson's definition provides a basis for examining the entire elder mistreatment phenomenon, it is too all-encompassing to meet the practical practitioner-oriented focus of this book. Therefore, in this book we consider only intentional family mediated elder abuse and neglect against competent elders and we modify her categories of mistreatment to be consistent with the practical approach relied on in this book:

Abuse: Intentional and Unintentional	*Neglect: Intentional and Unintentional*
psychological	psychological
physical	physical
financial	financial

Many researchers and practitioners have distinguished between unintentional (passive) neglect and intentional (active) neglect. An example of intentional or active neglect would include a caregiver who does not buy medications for an elderly relative after the physician has prescribed them. A caregiver who is unintentionally or passively neglectful would buy the medications but inadvertently administer the drugs incorrectly, resulting in harm to the older victim. It is not the intention of this caregiver to inflict injury, yet unintentional misinterpretation or inattention results in improper care. There has been little or no attention paid to unintentional abuse, and it is generally assumed that all abuse is intentional. This is not the case. For example, a mentally retarded son may hit his elderly mother to gain her attention when she's asleep, unwittingly causing her harm. (Since this book's focus is intentionally mediated family mistreatment against the elderly, we do not discuss unintentional abuse or neglect in detail.)

Psychological abuse. Psychological abuse encompasses a range of behaviors that cause emotional stress or injury to an older person. These behaviors include verbal abuse such as yelling, insults, and threatening remarks, as well as prolonged silence or ignoring an older person. One form of psychological abuse is infantilism—a form of ageism whereby the elderly individual is treated as a child. Infantilism patronizes the older person and may encourage passive acceptance of a dependent or victim role.

Physical abuse. Physical abuse refers to any bodily harm, contact, or injury inflicted by a relative on an older individual. This form of abuse includes striking, shoving, shaking, beating, or restraining. Sexual assault is included in this category and is a form of physical abuse requiring special emphasis here, as many workers find this form of violence inconceivable when an older individual is involved. Sexual abuse refers to any form of sexual intimacy without consent or through the use of force or the threat of force.

Financial abuse. Financial abuse includes all misappropriations of finances, as well as theft of property or possessions of an older individual. This form of abuse includes theft, "conning," and extortion.

Neglect—intentional and unintentional. There is only limited consensus about the definition of neglect. For example, some authors (Block & Sinnott, 1979; Phillips, 1983) include "intentional neglect" under the general category of "physical abuse," and keep "unintentional neglect" as its own category; other authors list intentional and unintentional neglect under the one heading "neglect."

One aspect of the definition of neglect on which there seems to be general agreement is that it is an act of omission, a "failure to provide some degree of minimal care for another individual"(Fulmer & Ashley, 1986). This is in contradistinction to abuse, which is an act of commission, or an act performed that harms another individual.

Self-neglect is another form of neglect that is of great concern to professionals; the term refers to an older person's failure to provide an adequate degree of care for him- or herself. This self-inflicted neglect may be intentional or unintentional. (Since this form of neglect is not inflicted by another family member, but rather is self-imposed, it will not be addressed in this book, either.)

Research has not yet identified behaviors that characterize neglect, making it difficult for the worker to differentiate between the presence or absence of this form of mistreatment (Fulmer & Ashley, 1986). Although potential indicators of neglect are often listed in other publications, Fulmer and Ashley emphasize that these are arbitrary lists, serving mainly to increase awareness about the issue. Another major problem, according to Fulmer and Ashley, is differentiating between the potential ravages of a disease process on an older person and changes that come about from neglect. Even in the absence of clearly defined indicators validated by research, detection of neglect is still possible, and is covered more fully in Chapter 3.

Further complicating the issue of neglect is the difficulty in determining who is responsible for the elder's care needs. For example: The worker who is assigned to help an older person with multiple health care problems, who is incapable of helping himself, may think that the daughter living nearby, who once provided daily assistance for her father but stopped without putting other services in place, should have been more responsible. Indeed, the worker may call the daughter "neglectful."

This outrage reflects the worker's own sense of right and wrong and of what familial obligations ought to be. But, legally, it would be difficult—if not impossible—in most states to prosecute the daughter. The laws governing this area are generally vague and do not specify the care responsibilities of family members for their older relatives, unless a relative is an older individual's guardian or other legal appointee. This is in contrast to "child neglect," in which a parent has the legal responsibility of care. Fulmer and Ashley's definition of neglect—the failure to provide some degree of minimal care for another person—implies responsibility, yet these obligations are not clearly delineated by law.

INCIDENCE OF ELDER MISTREATMENT AND CHARACTERISTICS OF VICTIMS AND PERPETRATORS

INCIDENCE

The epidemiology of elder abuse and neglect is better understood due to a survey by Pillemer and Finkelhor in 1986. The survey of 2,020 randomly selected elderly people living in the Boston metropolitan area found an incidence rate of mistreatment of 32 per 1,000 population for people over 65. The investigation looked at verbal abuse, neglect, and physical abuse. *Abuse* was defined as physical abuse, including hitting, slapping, or pushing; *neglect* was defined as depriving a person of something needed for daily living; and chronic *verbal aggression* was defined to include threats and insults.

CHARACTERISTICS OF
VICTIMS AND ABUSERS

The Pillemer and Finkelhor study found that most mistreatment is committed by one spouse against another: 65% of the abuse cases were between spouses and only 23% involved an adult offspring abusing a parent. Abused elderly were more likely to have poor health and live with someone else. Neglected elderly were more likely to live alone and to have fewer social supports than their nonabused elder counterparts. The study results also contradicted the previous impression that most elder abuse victims are women; in fact, elderly male spouses were actually twice as likely to be abused as female spouses. While more elderly husbands reported being abused by their wives, the wives reported more serious injuries when abused. Abuse was present at all economic levels and in all age groups among the elderly. Previous literature pointed to analogies between elder abuse and child abuse, yet this study suggested elder abuse to be more analogous to spouse abuse. Although this sample showed a high proportion of spouse perpetrators, it is important to note that the significant risk factor for abuse was shown to be the close proximity of living arrangements between victim and abuser and not their relationship.

Recently, Wolf et al. (1982) sought to identify characteristics of both victims and perpetrators of the various forms of elder mistreatment. The categories included were physical, psychological, and financial abuse, and intentional and unintentional neglect. The 328 victims included in the sample came from the three sites of the federally funded direct service programs called the Model Projects. Victims at the three sites were similar with regard to age, sex, marital status, living arrangements, and need for ambulatory devices. The only major difference was that one site's perpetrator group had a significantly younger average age when compared to the other two sites. The Model Projects study does not provide a conclusive profile but gives an important description of the characteristics of victims and perpetrators in a specific geographic population.

The Model Projects study showed that 56.5% of victims were 75 years old or over, 85% were female, 31% were married, 33.3% lived alone, and 53.5% required supportive devices for ambulation or were bedridden. The study also revealed 59.9% of perpetrators were younger than 60 years of age, 63.9% were males, and 74.3% lived with victims. Among perpetrators living with victims, 23% were sons, 18.5% were daughters, 17.9% were husbands, 6.8% were wives, 21% were other relatives, and 13.9% were nonrelatives.

Of the mistreatment documented in this study, the most prevalent form was psychological, which occurred in 72% of the cases; physical abuse occurred in 45.7%, financial abuse in 35.9%, unintentional neglect in 35.7%, and intentional neglect in 19.8% of the sample.

To develop victim and perpetrator profiles of the various kinds of mistreatment occurring in their sample, the authors of the Model Projects study analyzed data for the following factors: (a) age and marital status, (b) dependency status (specifically, the physical/functional status and psychological or cognitive status), and (c) social network features, such as availability of emergency contacts and recent loss of social supports. The following profiles emerged:

TABLE 1.1
Profiles of Victims and Perpetrators by Type of Maltreatment

	Physical Abuse	Psychological Abuse	Material Abuse	Active Neglect	Passive Neglect
Victim					
Sociodemography					
Age/Marital status	Younger/Married		Single		Older/Single
Dependency					
Physical/Functional status	More independent in IADL/ADL	More independent in IADL/ADL	Problems with finance management and transportation	Problems with IADL; dependent for ADL and companionship; need supportive devices	Problems with IADL; need for supportive devices; dependent in ADL and companionship
Psychological/Cognitive status	Poor emotional health	Poor emotional health; oriented in 3 spheres; no recent decline in mental status		Problems with orientation and memory	Recent decline in mental health; problems with orientation, memory and giving consent
Social network	Stable	Emergency contact	Recent loss of supports	No emergency contact	Loss of social supports
Perpetrator					
Sociodemography					
Age/Sex			Younger	Older/Female	

Living arrangements		Lives with victim	Does not live with victim		Lives with victim
Psychological status	History of mental illness; alcohol abuse; recent decline in mental status	History of mental illness; recent decline in mental status; unrealistic expectation of victim	Alcohol abuse: no recent decline in mental status	No history of mental illness	Realistic expectations
Dependency					
Physical status	Recent decline in health	Recent and long-term medical complaints	No recent medical complaints		Recent medical complaint
Dependency issues	Increased dependency		Financial dependency	No change in dependency	No financial dependency
Quality of relationship to victim	Poor	Poor			Good
Stress	No recent financial problems		Recent change in financial/job status; long-term and recent financial problems	Victim is a source of stress	Victim is a source of stress
Social network			No family available for support		Loss social supports

SOURCE: R.S. Wolf, M.A. Godkin, K.A. Pillemer, *Pride Institute Journal of Long-Term Home Health Care 5* (4), (Fall, 1986), pp. 14-15. Reprinted by permission.

POTENTIAL CAUSES AND RISK FACTORS
FOR ELDER MISTREATMENT

The following are factors that not only indicate increased risk for mistreatment but also incorporate various causation theories with regard to elder abuse and neglect. At present, there are only a small number of known risk factors, although, with additional research, other factors may become apparent. Pillemer (1986a) lists five risk factors that help to identify elder mistreatment: (1) psychopathology on the part of the abuser, (2) transgenerational violence, (3) dependency, (4) external stress, and (5) social isolation. Each of these factors will be examined in greater detail.

PSYCHOPATHOLOGY ON THE PART
OF THE ABUSER

Research indicated that many perpetrators of elder mistreatment have a history of hospitalization or mental illness (Wolf, 1986, pp. 218-238). Pillemer (1986a), in a matched sample, found perpetrators of physical elder abuse were more likely to have a history of mental illness and of alcohol abuse than the control group. Although sufficient research is not available to make a definitive statement, this is in striking comparison to the profile of younger spouse abusers, who tended to have no greater frequency of mental illness than their nonabusing counterparts (Gelles, 1974, pp. 190-204).

Concern about the perpetrator's psychiatric status is vital yet is not always considered by professionals doing assessments. When an adult child has a mental illness requiring inpatient psychiatric assistance, often the parents' home is the discharge site of last resort. Out of concern that a child will be homeless or have to stay at a shelter, parents frequently agree to take the dependent adult offspring into their home. With the trend toward "deinstitutionalization," it is imperative that mental health professionals discharging a dependent adult offspring to the parents' home be aware that the offspring may become abusive to his or her parents. Patients who are not violent within the institution may be violent in the home. Without carefully scrutinizing the potential for serious domestic conflict and making well-defined provisions for follow-up, it is possible to create a situation in which elder mistreatment is a certain outcome.

TRANSGENERATIONAL VIOLENCE

There is suspicion that in some cases of elder mistreatment the perpetrator was abused as a child, either by the elder victim or perhaps by the victim's spouse. In some elder mistreatment cases, there is a spirit of retaliation in response to this previous abuse. Some experts believe that because the abuser has experienced mistreatment, the violent behavior is transmitted transgenerationally and mirrors the manner in which the individual learned to express his or her own anger and frustration while "growing up."

This theory has been hard to substantiate for a number of reasons. First, victims who had been abusive in the past do not readily admit to this behavior, or they may not define their previous behavior as abusive or may not even remember it. Next, it may not have been the victim who was abusive, but the victim's spouse. In these cases, it may not be a matter of not remembering or minimizing past behavior, the elderly victim may not know that his or her spouse were an abuser. The mistreatment perpetrated by the adult child may have a spirit of retaliation but may be directed, in some cases, at the innocent parent. Pillemer (1986a) found no significant correlation between the history of abuse as a child and perpetuation of mistreatment as an adult; he states, however, that this area needs further research.

DEPENDENCY

Several studies have pointed out the financial dependency of the abuser on the victim (Hwalek, Sengstock, & Lawrence, 1984; Wolf, Godkin, & Pillemer, 1984). And, in a controlled study, Pillemer (1986a) found that physically abused elders were more likely to be depended upon by their perpetrators than to be dependent upon them. Pillemer and Finkelhor (1988), in the epidemiologic study described earlier, confirmed this. Their study also found that abusers were usually dependent in some way on the individual they abused. Pillemer (1986a) draws on social exchange theory and postulates that the socially unacceptable dependency of an adult offspring or relative on an older person leads to a feeling of powerlessness, with mistreatment occurring as an attempt "to compensate for this perceived loss of power." In some cases a mutual dependency exists. For example, an older person may be dependent on the abuser for socialization or for performing various activities of daily living, while the abuser may be dependent on the victim for housing and money.

EXTERNAL STRESS

There are some relatives who respond to the stress of delivering care by mistreating their dependent elder relative; often these relatives do not have the desire, inclination, knowledge, or financial and emotional resources to deliver care.

Family violence researchers report that financial problems, care-giving responsibilities, and other tensions may create frustration and anger that may be expressed by some people through acts of abuse (Strauss, Gelles, & Steinmetz, 1980). Also, if the dependent elder is unable to express appreciation and satisfaction, this tends to increase caregiver frustration. However, in most families that provide care for their elderly relatives, there is no violence or mistreatment, so external stress as a risk factor can only partially explain the elder abuse phenomenon.

ISOLATION

In other forms of domestic violence, such as child and spouse abuse, social isolation has been identified as a risk factor. Those families with friends or relatives in close proximity, and those who have frequent social interaction, appear to have a decreased incidence of family violence (Nye, 1979, pp. 1-41). One explanation is that those likely to abuse do not do so as much when there are others around to observe their behavior. Also, if caregiving stress is a factor, a strong support system may help to alleviate this problem.

Several studies have found that elder abuse victims have increased social isolation (Phillips, 1983; Pillemer, 1986a). Pillemer (1986a) tested the hypothesis that physically abused elder victims were more socially isolated than members of a matched control group. He found that, in addition to being more isolated than the control group, when social supports were present the victimized group was less satisfied with their supports than the nonvictimized group. This isolation may lead to increased victimization.

Each case of elder mistreatment must be carefully evaluated to see what risk factors are present and also if clear lines of etiology are apparent or if there is an overlap of causes, such as caregiver stress coexisting with transgenerational violence. These risk factors create a framework that can help guide intervention and thereby ensure a sense of the victim's safety. For example, intervention for a victim being abused by a drug addicted family member would be different from intervention for a recent stroke victim being abused by a relative experiencing over-whelming stress in providing care. For many elder abuse victims, their abusers are not caregivers but family members who often are dependent on the older relative for money, housing, and/or emotional support.

Chapter 3 reviews how to use these risk factors in the assessment of elder mistreatment.

Chapter 2

FRAMING THE PROBLEM
OF ELDER MISTREATMENT

with Karl Pillemer

Elder mistreatment has been identified as a significant social problem by both the aging service network and the domestic violence movement. Each perspective has contributed differently to the understanding of the phenomenon and, therefore, there is much to be gained by examining the interrelationship of the two. In addition, since elder mistreatment is perpetrated on people age 60 and over, a full understanding of this phenomenon requires insight into the issues surrounding aging.

The aging network responds to the needs of an over-60 population that is diverse in its physical and mental capacities. The services provided by this network typically include everything from home care and adult day care to protective services, job retraining, and health promotion programs. Professionals working with geriatric populations tend to be overexposed to those seniors with health problems, and less involved with the "well elder" population. As a result of this exposure to seniors requiring extensive care, this network has a tendency to view mistreatment as a result of "caregiver stress," and downplays the relationship of elder mistreatment to family violence.

This is unlike the population served by the domestic violence network that is primarily under age 60 with few chronic health problems. This network views its clientele as victims of violent crimes and its services reflect this. The services typically provided include emergency shelters

AUTHORS' NOTE: The collaborator for this chapter, Karl Pillemer, Ph.D., is Research Associate with the University of New Hampshire's Family Research Laboratory, Durham, New Hampshire.

and hot lines, criminal justice advocacy, and support group counseling. This network, however, is reluctant to work with older victims of domestic violence since it is generally unfamiliar with aging issues and has yet to develop sufficient services for people with disabilities. For example, there are few shelters that accommodate people with mobility impairments.

AGING NETWORK PERSPECTIVE

This perspective considers the demographics of aging, ageism, and myths concerning the process of aging.

DEMOGRAPHICS

There are many more people 65 and over today than in any other period of history. In 1900 the average life expectancy was 47. The average baby born today will live to the age of 74. In 1900, only 4% of the population was 65 and over; by 1980, 11% of Americans were that age. Experts predict that by 2030, 17% of the population will be over the age of 65.

In addition, the elderly population itself is getting older. The fastest-growing segment of the elderly population is the over-85 age group. In 1980, 9% of the 2.3 million elderly were over 65; in 2020, 8 million or 14.5% of the elderly will be over 85. Due to the large size of this segment of the population, which is unprecedented in the history of the world, this group will require increased care for their multiple medical and social needs, but to exactly what extent is unclear. The over-85 age group typically suffers from multiple chronic illnesses. In addition, it is anticipated that this increasing dependency creates the need for more social services (Watts & McCally, 1984).

The majority of America's 27 million population of elderly is female. It is therefore entirely correct to speak of the feminization of old age. In 1979, for every 100 women over the age of 65 there were 68.4 men. In the over-85 group, for every 100 women there were 44.7 men. This disproportion in survival between men and women is expected to increase even further by the year 2000. There is a racial disproportion in the elderly population as well. Whites outlive blacks, who outlive Hispanics.

The majority of old people are on fixed incomes and approximately one-quarter of our nation's older adults live at or below the poverty level. Although the financial position of older women living alone has improved greatly in recent years, almost half have median incomes of $5,000 a year or less. A total of 17% of American women over 65 have incomes below the poverty line, in contrast to 10% of the men.

With the increased number of the "old old" population (those age 75 and over, as opposed to the "young old," age 55 to 75), who tend to have one or more physical or mental impairments, there will be a greater need for domestic violence services to accommodate people with disabilities. Finally, those victims with limited financial resources cannot readily "purchase" safety. For example, a victim living on a small, fixed income cannot comfortably entertain the thought of moving, especially if a mortgage is already paid off or if the rent is low.

AGEISM

Ageism is a system of destructive, false beliefs about the elderly that has deep roots in our society (Butler, 1969). Specific ageist assumptions about older people are legion: "They can't hear. They can't remember. They can't think for themselves. They're depressing. They're non-productive. And they're infantile." These beliefs, until fairly recently, were the basis for mandatory retirement (Greene et al., 1986).

Health professionals in particular are more susceptible than the lay public to ageist assumptions. Their work often limits them to seeing the most ill, the most dependent, or the often demented older person. These professionals begin to generalize from this limited experience. They rarely see the robust "noninstitutionalized" elderly who function independently. Ageist attitudes are an occupational hazard for all health professionals.

Where do such ageist attitudes actually come from? Obviously, there are many sources, among them, fear of aging and one's own mortality. Fears of obsolescence, fears of physical losses in a society preoccupied with production, and certainly the youth-oriented "Pepsi generation" mentality promotes an ageist perspective. But the distinction to be noted about ageism is that, unlike sexism, racism, and other "isms," in which the focus of discrimination is on someone you will never become (a white person doesn't turn black, a man doesn't become a woman), ageism has a personal focus. If we are fortunate, we will all become elderly.

A poor understanding of the process of aging and negative attitudes toward aging may be important factors in the development of abusive and neglectful behaviors. Living in an ageist world in which negative

attitudes toward aging and old people are accepted creates an environment in which elder mistreatment may readily occur. For example,
societal ageism creates isolation of older people by preventing them
from participating in the work force. This undervaluing of older people
contributes to the development of low self-acceptance. Isolation is a risk
factor for elder mistreatment and low self-acceptance is an emotional
state that inhibits many victims from seeking help. These factors will be
discussed later in the book.

In addition, when elder abuse victims reach out for help, sometimes
workers assisting them respond in an ageist way. Two disconcerting
examples of ageist responses include the police officer who may
unquestioningly accept a relative's statement that an elderly person has
Alzheimer's disease and therefore does not intervene (believing the
stereotype that all people over the age of 65 have some form of
dementia), or the judge who dismisses a case because it is inconceivable
to him that an 80-year-old husband is capable of beating his 79-year-old
wife.

There is an abundance of myths concerning the process of aging that
often give rise to ageism:

Myth 1: Old age starts at 65. The reasons for considering age 65 as
marking the start of old age are mostly social custom rather than
biological fact. Different organ systems in one individual age at different
rates. For example, an individual may have supple and unwrinkled skin
yet have major kidney dysfunction. Since there is a great variation in the
rate of aging among individuals, chronological age is just not a precise
indicator of functional capacity. A life can be divided into stages. The
early stage of growth and development is marked by rapid increases in
cognitive development, physical maturation, and other capacities.
These then begin to peak in the late twenties and thirties (e.g., kidney
function, exercise capacity). Some functions then begin to decline, and
this continues into old age. The loss of functions is linear into the eighth
decade. The elderly simply have sustained greater functional losses due
to their longer lives, not a more rapid rate of deterioration.

The domestic violence network does not usually work with people
over 65. Yet this is an arbitrary cutoff. At this time, much of elder
mistreatment is spouse abuse. In some of the cases, the relationship has
been abusive for many years and continues past age 65. In other cases,
the onset of the abuse was in later years.

Myth 2: Old age and illness are synonymous. There is a popular
notion that aging is virtually synonymous with deterioration. For
example, 80% of those over 65 have one or more chronic diseases, and

50% of the aged have some limitation of activity. It's not surprising that the general public concludes that old age is to be dreaded. But, while large numbers of older people do have chronic illnesses, most appear to function quite well. Add to this the fact that 14% of the elderly have no chronic illnesses at all and the aging picture becomes less bleak.

Emphasis on deterioration leads to viewing old age as a state of illness and the elderly as passive and infantile, dependent upon the generosity of younger adults for support. That old age can be a state of wellness becomes, given this perspective, inconceivable. This wellness perspective is very distant from the medical model on which our health care system is built.

There is also a prevailing belief that disability is only a personal, individual problem. However, disability has environmental characteristics. Individuals may function poorly in an environment containing barriers to their vision or movement but may function without difficulty in an environment adapted to their needs. The older person who cannot climb stairs has no real disability in an elevator building. With attention to behavior modifications, motivational factors, and environmental adaptation, one can say that "aging" is malleable in many ways.

An understanding of normal aging is essential to enable the practitioner to differentiate between normal aging and possible mistreatment. If illness is thought of as synonymous with age, then the opportunity to evaluate mistreatment as an underlying problem is missed. For example, if a health practitioner accepts unquestioningly that an elderly person's hip fracture was a result from either a fall or osteoporosis, perceived to be part of normal aging, then questions about possible mistreatment won't be asked.

Myth 3: Old age is synonymous with senility. The fear of mental decline is, unfortunately, a major concern for older people. Yet only a small number of elderly develop dementia. There are many different causes for mental deterioration. If the worker expects older people to become senile, then possible forms of reversible dementia go undetected.

Protectionist attitudes toward elderly victims of family mistreatment are widely held by professionals. For example, when an older person decides to remain in an abusive environment, it is often assumed that she or he would make this decision only if judgmentally impaired. From this assumption, workers often request mental status exams and often recommend nursing home placement. These protective attitudes toward old people derive from an underlying paternalism; but most old people, like their younger counterparts, are capable of making decisions for themselves. In addition, since elder mistreatment can cause a profound depression that may mimic dementia, it is critical that a proper mental status assessment be conducted before claiming an older person incompetent. If the underlying depression is treated, mental function can return.

Myth 4: Old people are all the same. Nothing could be farther from the truth, yet stereotyping brings people to think that as old people become older, they look and think alike. Of course, there is an enormous diversity in the backgrounds, careers, personal styles, and financial statuses of older people, just as there is with the general population. Indeed, due to the range of their experience, there may be even greater differences among older individuals than among younger individuals.

Also, when we think about the "elderly," we have to differentiate between "young old" and "old old." Someone at 20 is a different person in many ways from who he or she will be 30 years later. Similarly, someone at 90 is different from who he or she was at 60.

Furthermore, persons who reach 65 today have had different life experiences than the generation that preceded them. Specific historical circumstances have shaped their formative and adult years, such as war and economic depression. So each birth cohort has a different set of experiences and characteristics as well as similarities. For example, individuals who are entering their sixties now often have a different concept of what the physician is and what their approach to him or her should be than did those in their sixties two decades ago. Many patients who are now in their eighties grew up with the idea of the doctor as a god; as a result, often they won't ask questions, as younger patients do. Similarly, those in their eighties now may have misconceptions about what counseling is, as their generation did not participate in psychotherapy as freely as younger generations do today.

DOMESTIC VIOLENCE PERSPECTIVE

To accurately discuss the domestic violence perspective on elder mistreatment, it is necessary to review how it is similar to and different from other forms of domestic violence, specifically the abuse of children and violence against women. Since "hard" research in this area is lacking, this analysis can be regarded only as suggestive, rather than definitive (Finkelhor & Pillemer, 1984).

ELDER ABUSE COMPARED
WITH CHILD ABUSE

Elder abuse is more frequently compared to child abuse than to spouse abuse within the context of family violence. This is due to the conceptualization of elder abuse as a problem of "caregiving." Many cases in which a very dependent and frail elderly person is abused by his or her caretaker take on a parent-child character. That is, the extreme dependency of the older person is treated as analogous to the dependency of small children on their parents. The dynamic in such situations is presumed to be that of an overburdened caretaker who is unprepared for the stress of having to care for a relative and who, in frustration, lashes out at the elder (Steinmetz & Anderson, 1983).

Both elder abuse and child abuse came to the public's attention in roughly the same manner. They were first identified by professionals: nurses, social workers, lawyers, doctors. These professionals publicized the problem, sought funds for intervention programs, and testified in favor of mandatory reporting and protective services legislation (Salend, Kane, Satz, & Pynoos, 1984). Further, public welfare agencies have generally been designated to deal with elder abuse. In fact, in some states the agencies that handled child abuse cases were also given responsibility for intervening in elder abuse.

Because of these factors, there has been a tendency to look at elder abuse as having the same causes and dynamics as child abuse. But this parallel is in fact fundamentally flawed. First, much elder abuse *does not* occur by a caretaker against a dependent victim. In fact, over the past few years, research has shown that *the abuser is often the dependent one,* not the victim. For example, a young son with a drug abuse problem may return to the parents' home and wind up exploiting and inflicting violence on them. A child who has remained unhealthily dependent on his or her parents may come to resent them deeply. In such cases, the abuse may not be in reaction to the responsibilities of caretaking, but may be a rebellion against the position of dependency (see Pillemer, 1986a; Wolf & Pillemer, in press). Such a conceptualization is consistent with research on family violence (Finkelhor, 1983).

Even when the elderly person is dependent, the conditions of dependency are quite different from those of children. Parents have a clear legal responsibility for children, unlike almost all of the caregivers to the elderly, who have no such role. Unless proven otherwise by complicated legal and psychiatric means, older people are considered to be competent, responsible individuals, and are therefore responsible for decisions regarding their own welfare. Further, most elderly persons do not live with their children, and any remaining social expectations that they should do so are rapidly disappearing. Based on this point alone, it is erroneous to equate the situation of elderly victims of domestic violence with those of abused children.

ELDER ABUSE COMPARED
WITH SPOUSE ABUSE

From a domestic violence perspective, it is easier to compare elder abuse to spouse abuse, since a considerable proportion of elder abuse *is* spouse abuse, which in some cases may have been occurring in the relationship for many years. The abuser was a spouse in 58% of the cases, and a child or other person in only 42% of the cases in one recent random-sample survey (Pillemer & Finkelhor, in press). The possibility that spousal violence is the predominant form of elder abuse mandates the need to consult research on spouse abuse in our attempts to understand mistreatment of the elderly.

When looking at elder abuse as similar to spouse abuse, we cease to adopt ageist attitudes toward the elderly and recognize that many elderly are relatively independent, responsible adults. Such a perspective emphasizes the initiatives elder abuse victims can take on their own behalf. It also recognizes the by now commonly accepted research finding that many abusers are dependent on their victims.

IMPLICATIONS

There are insights to be gained from considering elder abuse as a form of domestic violence, although, at present, these comparisons remain speculative and require careful empirical investigation. Based on the existing evidence, the parallel between elder abuse and child abuse has been overdrawn. Elder abuse does not conform to the child abuse model in many ways, and the older victim's relationship to the abuser is not similar to the relationship between a child victim and abuser.

The comparison to spouse abuse does present identification and intervention strategies, such as those adopted from the battered women's movement. For example, as is detailed later in this book, self-help groups, in which victims come together to support each other, have great potential to assist victims of elder mistreatment. Such groups can allay the sense of stigma and self-blame of victims, and can help them to develop strategies for dealing with their abusers.

Similarly, the comparison to battered women suggests that emergency shelters and safe houses would be useful for elder abuse victims. There is some evidence that nursing homes are an all too frequent "solution" to elder mistreatment situations. A shelter differs radically from a nursing home in that it is temporary and assumes that the victim will return to living in the community after having the opportunity to escape the abuser.

Finally, the parallel to spouse abuse argues for the use of criminal sanctions in cases of elder abuse. Such intervention may reduce the revictimization of elderly persons. Victim assistance programs—which typically provide crisis intervention counseling, home lock replacement and repair, and advocacy—would also be useful in this effort.

It is clear that additional research is needed to establish the ways in which elder abuse and neglect is similar to other forms of domestic violence, and areas in which it is unique. Perhaps the most important point is the need for recognition that elder abuse and neglect is not necessarily—and probably not primarily—a problem of caregiving. It must also be seen as a form of domestic violence, no less than the battering of women and the mistreatment of children.

Chapter 3

DETECTION

It is a clinical impression that elder mistreatment tends to escalate in incidence and severity over time. The earlier it is identified, therefore, the greater the opportunity to intervene before abuse reaches extreme levels of severity and causes serious physical injury or death. In this chapter we will outline barriers to the detection of elder mistreatment, review key risk factors and indicators, and, through case examples, illustrate the four types of mistreatment defined in Chapter 1.

BARRIERS TO DETECTION

There are many barriers to the identification of elder mistreatment. These include victim denial of mistreatment, shame or fear of retaliation, victim isolation, lack of protocol development, ageist attitudes, and lack of knowledge on the part of professionals.

PROTOCOL DEVELOPMENT

Since few victims come forward and make clear statements about mistreatment, professionals need to be methodical and observant in their interviews and medical examinations in order to detect mistreatment situations. Obvious as well as less blatant indicators, such as confusion and unexplained paranoia, must be understood and looked for. Although a growing number of social service agencies and hospitals have developed detection guidelines or "protocols" for staff to follow when working with older adults, most have not. Consequently, many cases of elder mistreatment continue to go undetected.

Often professionals are likely to assist victims who come forward, but resist active measures to detect mistreatment. This is because few agencies have developed "intervention protocols," leaving many workers feeling unprepared and overwhelmed when a potential elder abuse victim is identified. Workers report feeling fearful that the abused elder might suffer severe harm or death because they did not respond swiftly and correctly. Similarly, they are concerned for their own safety when involved in these cases, and rightly so. Indeed, police for example, are more likely to be seriously hurt or killed when responding to domestic violence calls than any other crime scenario.

Workers also worry about civil or criminal liability for any mishandled cases, knowing full well that these cases tend to be among the most time-consuming, complex, and demanding. As in other areas of domestic violence or health care, workers have been sued, albeit infrequently. Workers might consider obtaining a professional insurance policy, often offered by professional associations, and be familiar with their organization's policy, if it has one, in handling lawsuits brought against staff.

Detection and intervention protocols help to minimize worker's fears and anxieties because they clarify agency expectations, thereby addressing in advance fears of liability that may be inhibiting the detection of abusive situations (Legal Research and Services to the Elderly, 1979).

The Harborview Medical Center in Seattle has developed an elder abuse protocol that is used in its emergency room. It is included (Appendix A) to give readers an example of the elements of a protocol. The Harborview instrument is one of the most thorough and usable protocols available, although it raises some conceptual concerns. For example, it uses the term *caregiver* when referring to the abuser. This creates "semantic" confusion, because many times the abuser is not a caregiver and, often, is actually dependent on the elder victim him- or herself for care and support. Each organization needs to adapt existing materials and create new ones in order to develop protocols suitable for its own setting and that fit its conceptualization of elder mistreatment.

AGEISM

Older people are frequently thought of as being frail, dependent, forgetful, and unable to determine what is in their own best interest. As mentioned in Chapter 1, these negative attitudes adversely affect the ability of professionals to detect mistreatment situations.

Case Illustration

The following case example illustrates the way a worker might be influenced by such negative perceptions of the elderly.

Mr. S, 95 years old, and his 35-year-old great-grandson went to the city's office in charge of heating complaints. Mr. S's heat had been turned off weeks before and he was worried about not having it with the cold months of winter ahead. The city worker addressed her question to the great-grandson, ignoring Mr. S completely. In fact, she went as far as asking the great-grandson to step inside her office, leaving Mr. S alone in the waiting area. The worker never talked with Mr. S directly.

Before leaving, Mr. S asked to speak with the supervisor and told her his story. Otherwise, no one would have discovered that the great-grandson had been responsible for, but negligent in, paying the bills. When her supervisor asked the worker why she never spoke to Mr. S directly, she explained that she thought he looked "too old" to communicate clearly. Upon further investigation, it was discovered that the great-grandson had used a good deal of Mr. S's savings to buy things for himself.

LACK OF KNOWLEDGE

In order to identify elder abuse victims, professionals need to be educated in the issues surrounding aging, domestic violence, and elder mistreatment. At present, most social service workers, health care providers, and criminal justice personnel have not been suitably trained on these topics. Some of these workers expect abuse and neglect to be apparent or that a person being abused will simply mention this should it be serious enough to warrant attention. They are unaware that most elder abuse victims are too ashamed or humiliated to talk about their problem, might fear retaliation if they did summon help, and often minimize the seriousness of their situation.

ISOLATION

An individual's isolation tends to increase with age due to one or more of the following factors: retirement, loss of friends or relatives through death or relocation, increased disabilities limiting mobility, and the fear of street crime. Recent research indicates that elder abuse victims tend to be more isolated than their nonabused elder counterparts (Pillemer, 1986a). It is not known if victims are more isolated than nonvictims prior to the onset of abuse, or if they become isolated because of the abuse. It is known, however, that many abusers limit the victim's access to the outside world. Examples of this include refusing the victim use of the telephone, denying visitors entry into the house, and accompanying the victim on all errands.

It may be that there is a "cycle of violence" in which a victim is isolated, abuse begins, and this in turn further increases the isolation (Pillemer, 1986b). In such cases, opportunities for detection occur in the health care setting or upon a home visit by visiting nurses, social workers, or other professionals. These may be the few instances that the victim has contact with outsiders.

But very often when a professional tries to interact with the victim, a younger relative or caregiver is present. It is not unusual for a professional to speak to the accompanying younger individual, excluding the older person entirely. Therefore, workers should first interview the older person privately, and then immediately interview the accompanying relative separately (Quinn & Tomita, 1986). It is important to observe how the older person and relative relate, the dynamics of their communication, and their individual roles in relation to each other, with an eye to the possible existence of abuse. In the next section, a list of indicators of elder mistreatment is provided to help workers with this evaluation.

RISK FACTORS

Research on elder mistreatment has not yet uncovered what actually causes abuse and neglect. Research has, however, identified some major factors that, when present, can inform workers which elderly are at high risk of mistreatment. The evaluation of these risk factors described in Chapter 1, in the handling of each case, will enable the worker to assess the degree of a potentially abusive situation.

> *Risk Factor 1: Psychopathology on the part of the abuser.* Do any of the children or other relatives in contact with the elder have a history of mental illness? Is there a tendency toward the acting out of aggression by adult children or other relatives in contact with the older individual? Are there signs of alcohol and/or drug abuse or misuse?
>
> *Risk Factor 2: Transgenerational violence.* Is there any past history of violence in the family?
>
> *Risk Factor 3: Dependency.* Is there an adult child or other relative in the home dependent on the older person for income, shelter, or emotional support?
>
> *Risk Factor 4: Stress.* Have any stressful life events recently occurred, for example, loss of a job, moving, death of a significant other? Is there chronic financial stress? Who is providing care in the household? Who is experiencing "caregiver stress"—the older person or the abusing relative?

Risk Factor 5: Isolation. Is the older person satisfied with the amount and quality of contact with family, friends, and neighbors? Does the older person have the opportunity to pursue interests outside the home? If there has been a change in a pattern of pursuing outside activities, is the older person satisfied with this change?

Most studies have found that elders are more likely to be abused by people with whom they are living (Pillemer & Finkelhor, 1988). We have, therefore, added this as a risk factor.

Risk Factor 6: Living arrangements. Does the older person share his or her own house or apartment with a relative? Or does the older person live with a family in their house or apartment?

INDICATORS OF MISTREATMENT

The following details possible indicators for each type of mistreatment and provides a case illustration for each. Although, to date, research has not identified specific indicators of mistreatment, it is our clinical experience that these indicators, when manifested, prove to be clues to underlying mistreatment.

As discussed in Chapter 1, the categories of mistreatment addressed in this book are intentional psychological, physical, and financial abuse and neglect. Abuse is an act of commission while neglect is an act of omission. Often the resulting pain and damage are indistinguishable.

In each case of mistreatment, several forms of abuse may be present. For example, it would be unlikely for physical abuse to occur without concomitant psychological abuse. In addition, the presence of any one of the indicators discussed below does not necessarily point to abuse; rather, it is the clustering of multiple indicators that suggests the possibility of underlying abuse or neglect. Also, workers need to respect cultural differences so that their behavioral norms are not projected onto their clients. For example, some families yell loudly at each other, indicating to some outsiders disrespect, yet to the members of the family this may be acceptable behavior.

PSYCHOLOGICAL ABUSE AND NEGLECT

Psychological abuse induces mental and emotional distress in the victim. Examples of this type of mistreatment include threatening remarks or insults, harsh commands, isolating the victim from social contact, or treating the older person as being invisible by consistently

TABLE 3.1

Possible Indicators of Psychological Mistreatment

- insomnia, sleep deprivation, or need for excessive sleep
- change in appetite
- unusual weight gain or loss
- tearfulness
- unexplained paranoia
- low self-acceptance
- excessive fears
- ambivalence
- confusion
- resignation
- agitation

NOTE: These indicators may also be present in physical and financial, abusive and neglectful situations.

ignoring their concerns and comments. Possible indicators of this type of mistreatment are included in Table 3.1.

Case Illustration

The following case example illustrates psychological abuse and is followed by an analysis.

The senior center director noticed that Mrs. K, age 69, a regular member, had become ravenous during lunch, helping herself to several servings and still wanting more. This went on for a couple of weeks. Worried about Mrs. K's health, the director invited her into the office to talk. The director shared with Mrs. K what she had observed and inquired about her health and well-being. Mrs. K denied that she was eating more than usual at lunch and explained that she had just had a physical and was given a clean bill of health. Thanking the director for her concern, Mrs. K left the office.

Mrs. K's behavior continued and the director inquired several times as to how she was feeling. Finally, Mrs. K told the director that her son had been having problems and could be quite nasty at times. She also said that once he had threatened to poison her food, making her frightened to eat at home. She said she wanted to find him help, claiming he had always been a "smart boy" and would be okay if someone just talked to him about getting his life in order.

Analysis

Many abusers threaten their victims, making it difficult for the victims to conduct daily activities and jeopardizing their health. In this example, Mrs. K could not eat without fearing she would be poisoned. Yet often the victims respond with love and concern for the abuser, feeling the main problem is the abuser's mental health and not the results of the abuse. Victims set out on a search for help for their abusive relatives, and since they are worried that outsiders will judge the relative harshly, go to great lengths to impress others that the abuser is a good albeit troubled person.

This example also illustrates that it frequently takes persistence on the part of a provider before a victim will talk about his or her problems. Mrs. K finally shared her fears and concerns only after repeated overtures by the director.

PHYSICAL ABUSE AND NEGLECT

Physical abuse and neglect produce a wide range of bodily injuries. Examples of this type of mistreatment include hitting, punching, shaking, slapping, sexual assault, use of a weapon, and not feeding properly or providing necessary medications. Possible indicators of this type of mistreatment are outlined in Table 3.2.

Case Illustration

The following case example illustrates physical abuse and is followed by an analysis.

Mr. C, a 70-year-old, middle-class man, came to the agency seeking assistance for his daughter, a 35-year-old drug abuser. Mr. C was visibly distressed, his eyes were teary, he was shaking, and he moved around uncomfortably in his chair. He looked exhausted and when the worker asked him if he had had any sleep, he slowly shook his head and admitted his daughter had kept him up for two nights in a row, jabbing him with a letter-opener and burning him with cigarettes. He slowly rolled up his sleeve and there was a series of round red burns on his arm.

TABLE 3.2
Possible Indicators of Physical Mistreatment

- bruises
- welts
- lacerations
- punctures
- fractures
- burns
- signs of hair pulling, e.g., hemorrhaging below scalp
- unexplained venereal disease or other unexplained genital infections
- signs of physical confinement, e.g., rope burns
- malnutrition and/or dehydration, e.g., dry skin, sunken eyes, loss of weight
- soiled clothing or bed linens
- hyperthermia or hypothermia
- signs of excess drugging, lack of medication, or other misuse, e.g., decreased alertness, responsiveness, and orientation
- absence of eyeglasses, hearing aids, dentures, or prostheses
- unexpected or unexplained deterioration of health
- decubitus ulcers (pressure sores)

Analysis

In order to detect child abuse, pediatricians, pediatric nurses, and social workers have had to become familiar with the various indicators of that abuse. The same is true now for elder mistreatment.

In Mr. C's case, the worker was alerted to the presence of cigarette burns by the victim. In many other cases, however, victims do not disclose the abusive situation. Frequently, the signs are not clear and the worker must be sensitive to the range of potential indicators and must learn to explore any signs of distress that surface during the interview.

Mr. C's signs of distress were tearfulness and exhaustion. The worker targeted questions accordingly and the burns were discovered. But even obvious signs of physical abuse may be misdiagnosed without a high index of awareness on the part of the worker. For example, an older person may arrive at the emergency room of a hospital and be found to have a hip fracture. Medical personnel seldom probe into the specifics related to the injury if the victim is an older person. Often they rely on the report given by the person escorting the injured person to the hospital. This person may, in fact, be the abuser. A hip fracture could easily be misattributed to a fall when indeed the etiology was very different.

Case Illustration

The following case example illustrates physical neglect and is followed by an analysis.

> Mr. Z, age 83, was diagnosed with Alzheimer's disease while in a local hospital. Prior to his mental deterioration, he assigned his daughter durable power-of-attorney. The hospital discharged Mr. Z to his daughter's care after ascertaining that she was to hire her husband, using her father's money, as his home attendant. Mr. Z was to live in an apartment adjacent to their residence.

> On a follow-up visit several months after discharge, Mr. Z's physician was alarmed at his patient's rapidly deteriorating health, manifested by increased confusion, severe weight loss, difficulty ambulating, and questionable dehydration. Upon investigation, it was found that the son-in-law had not been following through with his responsibilities and had gone on winter vacation with his wife, leaving Mr. Z alone without heat, hot water, and food. The physician suspected that the daughter was abusing her responsibilities, spending the money on her own needs and deliberately neglecting those of her father.

Analysis

The intentionally neglectful caregiver is conscious of the potential results of specific behaviors. Mr. Z's daughter and son-in-law deliberately deceived the hospital into thinking they would deliver proper care. Cases in which there is unexpected or unexplained health deterioration should be flagged by workers, indicating that an investigation of a client's environmental circumstances is necessary. Mr. Z's physician was alerted by his patient's dramatic decline in health status and proceeded to explore the cause of this problem. However, the fact that the physician knew Mr. Z's daughter had durable power-of-attorney should have prompted him to an earlier follow-up.

FINANCIAL ABUSE AND NEGLECT

Financial abuse or neglect is the misuse or exploitation of, or inattention to, an older person's possessions and/or funds. Forms of this

TABLE 3.3
Possible Indicators of Financial Mistreatment

- unexplained or sudden inability to pay bills
- unexplained or sudden withdrawal of money from accounts
- disparity between assets and satisfactory living conditions
- lack of receptivity by older person or relative to any necessary
  assistance requiring expenditure, when finances are not a problem
- extraordinary interest by family member in older person's assets

type of mistreatment include conning or threatening the victim into handing over assets, abusing or neglecting the legal responsibility to manage the victim's money, and stealing possessions and cash. Possible indicators of financial mistreatment are outlined in Table 3.3

Case Illustration

The following case example illustrates financial abuse and is followed by an analysis.

Mrs. J, age 90, relied heavily on her son in helping her manage her finances after her husband died. Her husband had dealt with the family's finances all of their lives and she was too overwhelmed to start learning about such matters. Her son suggested she take all of her money, about $100,000, out of her various bank accounts and place it in an account in his name. He explained that he would be able to keep track of it better that way and whenever she wanted any of the money, she was to specify the amount and he would authorize payment. Mrs. J proceeded to do what was requested of her, keeping only one account in her own name. After the money was entrusted to her son, she never heard from him again. Embarrassed to tell anyone, it wasn't until her daughter found her mother's bank records that the abuse became known.

Analysis

This example illustrates the shame victims feel after a close relative betrays their trust. Mrs. J was so humiliated that she suffered her loss silently. It also exemplifies the dependency of some older people on others for financial management. This may be particularly true for older women, since financial matters were traditionally the man's purview. When widowed and confronted with investment responsibilities, many feel at a complete loss, a situation that leaves them vulnerable to exploitation by those feigning concern.

Some people who feel incapable of or inadequate in handling their own finances assign a *power-of-attorney*. This is a legal option that allows an individual to appoint another person to administer transactions. The power-of- attorney can be designed to fit the individual's specific needs. It can merely apply to one bank account or extend to the selling of stocks and real estate and the use of bank account funds. The power-of-attorney is appointed voluntarily by the individual and goes into effect immediately, but it can be easily revoked. A disadvantage is that the named agent is only accountable to the person requesting the power-of-attorney, setting the stage for abuse to occur without evoking the suspicion of anyone. Should the individual entrusted with the power-of-attorney become judgmentally impaired, it becomes void.

A *durable power-of-attorney* is a legal option similar in scope to the power-of-attorney. The difference is that it takes effect only when the person authorizing its use loses the capacity to make decisions regarding his or her financial affairs. (It is important to note that the power-of-attorney and durable power-of-attorney cannot be relied on for appointing someone to make health care decisions, as this appointment may not stand up in court.)

It is also possible for an older person to designate a *representative payee*. This is an individual or organization appointed to manage a person's social security, veteran's pension, or railroad retirement benefits. Once established, the beneficiary's wishes as to how to spend this money may not always be taken fully into account, leaving the door open for misuse and exploitation of the funds. Therefore, workers should consider the need for this arrangement carefully before advocating it.

Some people are no longer capable of managing their own finances because of cognitive impairment. These people may be appointed a *conservator* or *guardian* by the court. This is usually initiated by the family, a friend, or the state. The conservator has complete responsibility for all financial matters concerning the ward's estate. This is broader than the powers of the representative payee. Once a conservator is appointed, the ward is less likely to have his or her requests directly heard by the court if there is disagreement over how finances are spent. Guardianship is more expansive than conservatorship and includes responsibility for all finances and personal affairs, including decisions regarding contracts, hospitalization, and the course of medical treatment. The all-inclusive nature of conservatorship and guardianship leaves the ward vulnerable to abuse and exploitation if those responsible for care are not honest and trustworthy.

Please note that laws regarding powers-of-attorney, representative payees, and conservatorships and guardianships differ from state to state. It is not surprising that workers investigating financial abuse often need the consultation and assistance of an attorney to determine whether or not financial abuse has occurred and how to rectify the situation if damage was done.

Chapter 4

ASSESSMENT

Once a victim of elder mistreatment is detected, the worker must determine the needs of that person and the resources and supports available to assist him or her. The primary step is to understand the victim's thoughts and feelings concerning the abusive situation. The next step is to investigate the dimensions of the case, including victim health status, the availability of a support system, and community resources. This ongoing process is called "assessment" and usually continues into the "intervention" phase.

UNDERSTANDING THE VICTIM

To better understand elder mistreatment victims, we suggest that readers participate in the following imagery exercise adapted from one developed at the Rape Crisis Program of St. Vincent's Hospital in New York City. Two participants are necessary to do the exercise.

EXERCISE: IMAGINE SOMEONE YOU KNOW

Instructions: While one participant closes his or her eyes and listens, the other should read the following slowly.

> "Imagine a person you love who is 15 years old or older.... What does this person look like? . . . What does this person look like when he or she is smiling? . . . What do you wish for this person? . . . What is it about this person that you love? . . . What activity do you enjoy doing together? . . . What is your fondest memory of this person?

AUTHORS' NOTE: The section on abusers was written in collaboration with Pamela Ansell, M.S.W., Elder Abuse Specialist and Clinical Consultant, New York City.

"Now, imagine this person slapping your face. . . .What are you thinking?
. . . What are you feeling? . . . Do you feel shocked? Angry? Concerned? . . .
What are you going to do? . . . and, whom do you tell? . . . Open your eyes."

Participants should now discuss their thoughts and feelings. The
following questions are offered as a guide to the discussion.

(1) Was it hard to imagine this loved one slapping you? Why or why not?
(2) What were you thinking? That this is absurd? This could never happen?
That your loved one must be very upset or disturbed in order for this to
happen? That your loved one needs help? That you need help?
(3) What were you feeling? Shock? Anger? Resignation? Concern? Shame?
Guilt?
(4) Whom would you turn to for help? The police? Family? Friends? A
doctor? A social worker? Clergy? Or would you not confide in anyone,
preferring to try to discuss the problem privately with your loved one?
Would you fight back?

This is not the way elder mistreatment situations normally arise. For
elder mistreatment victims, things are not moving along calmly and
then suddenly there is a slap in the face. Of course, this is only an
exercise and participants may have had to force an image. Nonetheless,
it may provide a deeper insight into the thoughts and emotions of a
victim.

Usually when violence first occurs, many victims do not immediately
run to the police, to a social worker, or to their clergy. If there is serious
injury, victims may see a doctor, but many do not disclose the
mistreatment.

Many of the victims experience disbelief. They do not expect to be
mistreated by their children, their grandchildren, their nieces or
nephews, or spouses, the people they love.

On the other hand, some victims have been mistreated for many
years, often by their spouses. It is only because they are now 60 years of
age or older that the violence is termed "elder abuse." Or some may have
been victims of child abuse. Sadly, these victims, all too familiar with
family violence, expect it. Indeed, some of these victims cannot even
imagine a life without mistreatment.

ACCESS

The degree to which a thorough assessment can be made depends on
the worker's access to the victim and the abuser. In some cases, access is

not a problem because the victim desires assistance and the abuser does not restrict, or only mildly restricts, outside contact.

In other cases, the victim or the abuser might not talk openly with the worker making the assessment. Victims are often reluctant to discuss the problem of mistreatment with anyone and might deny the existence of abuse completely, to other people and sometimes even to themselves. In other cases the victim might be restricted by the abuser from having contact with outside agencies or individuals. For example, the abuser might intimidate the victim by making sure to be present during all interviews, might screen all phone calls and mail, or might refuse to give the worker entry to the residence.

The first step in the assessment process, then, is to determine what, if any, barriers there are to access. The worker should ask the following questions: What types of attempts at access have been made by phone? By mail? By home visit? Were the attempts thwarted and by whom? Has someone other than the worker tried to gain access to help with the assessment, for example, a friend, relative, neighbor, police? If so, what were the results of those attempts?

Attempts at access need to be tailored to each individual case and the success will depend on the degree of resistance on the part of the abuser and the victim. Approaches to gain access encompass a range of options. Trusted family and neighbors may have influence, and sometimes this trust can be "transferred" to the worker by associating with these individuals. The following case example illustrates this possibility.

Case Illustration

An Adult Protective Service worker responded to a call by a social worker to investigate a suspected case of physical abuse. She knocked on the apartment door, a voice of an older man answered weakly, and the worker identified herself. A woman's voice yelled out, "Go away!" The worker tried to talk with them through the door, but they no longer answered. She slipped her card under the door, and said if anyone needed help, to call her. As she was walking down the hallway to leave, a neighbor from across the hall stopped her.

The worker identified herself, and the neighbor confided that she had been friendly with the Johnsons for years, especially Mr. Johnson. She added that both Mr. and Mrs. Johnson had become reclusive over the last few months and she was concerned about them. When the worker expressed her interest in meeting with the Johnsons, the neighbor said that the best bet would be to come to the apartment on Tuesdays or Wednesdays in the morning, when Mrs. Johnson goes to work. She added, "With Mrs. Johnson there, that door will never open!" The worker asked if the neighbor would be around on Tuesday, and suggested that they both go to the door together.

Some abusers and victims respond to police authority and freely give the worker, accompanied by the police, access. And there are circumstances when the police may get access by posing "under cover." The following case example illustrates this possibility.

Case Illustration

A social worker at a community-based agency received a panicked phone call from the grandson of a 70-year-old woman. He claimed that his grandmother was being held captive inside her own apartment by his father. He stated that his father periodically tied her to a chair and would beat her, steal her money, and lock her inside the apartment. Also, he claimed that his father had served time for rape and had illegal possession of a gun.

The social worker deemed the situation too dangerous to make a routine home visit. She phoned the police precinct about the case and they confirmed that the alleged abuser had served time for rape by checking his name on the computer. Two police officers went in plain clothes to the apartment. They knocked on the door and the alleged abuser spoke with them through the door. The police officers said that they were community volunteers associated with the "Block Watch" program and that there had been a wave of burglaries in the building. They claimed to be providing all residents with information on the burglaries and giving advice on ways to further secure apartments. The alleged abuser let them in, and while one of the officers kept him occupied with the evaluation of the apartment's security, the other talked with the grandmother about her grandson's allegations.

Some workers may be concerned about the deception inherent in this type of investigation. There are many cases in which workers must balance the importance of gaining access against unorthodox methods that contain elements of deceit and manipulation.

In some circumstances workers may have reason to believe that an older person is in imminent danger of harm or death at the hand of a relative. In some states, there is legal recourse: The courts can order the family members to cooperate in an investigation, and, if they refuse, they can be held in contempt of court.

In general, the key to gaining access is through a thorough understanding of available options, persistence, and tenacity. There are cases in which the family provided access because the worker went to the door every day for weeks showing concern by leaving a note offering assistance. In some of these cases, the family opened the door to the worker because they were won over by the worker's demonstrated commitment.

DENSITY AND INTENSITY

In Chapter 1 we discussed Johnson's concepts of density and intensity as elements of the definition of elder mistreatment. As part of the assessment, the worker should determine the density of mistreatment or how many types of abuse are occurring (i.e., physical, psychological, financial, and neglect). The worker should also assess the frequency and severity of this abuse, that is, its intensity. (Workers might find it helpful to follow the assessment guidelines outlined in Appendix A.)

The density can be ascertained by asking the victim and, with the victim's permission, other family and friends not suspected of mistreatment what has occurred. Have signs or symptoms of psychological, physical, or financial abuse, or intentional neglect, been observed or witnessed first hand? What precisely was noticed? Or has the victim spoken to friends or family about mistreatment? If so, what was said? Often persistence and patience are required in order to gather accurate information. The victim, family, and friends may feel more comfortable with a worker after repeated contact. Often, workers are put in the position of having to do quick assessments because of time constraints. This is unfortunate, because in many cases the mistreatment pattern only becomes evident to others by observing over a period of time. As in most aspects of assessment and intervention, trust is the essential ingredient and must be built over time.

The intensity can be assessed by asking the victim and family and friends not suspected of mistreatment how often mistreatment occurs and how severe the damage is. For example, if physical abuse is a problem, ask: "How often does your relative hurt you?" (For psychological abuse, ask: "How often are you intimidated by your relative?" Or, for financial abuse, ask: "How often does your relative take your money?") This direct questioning may illicit inaccurate information if the victim minimizes the seriousness of the problem or is too fearful or ashamed to tell what is happening. By talking with family and friends, with the victim's permission, the worker has a better chance of obtaining a more accurate picture.

It is also important to assess if the mistreatment has increased in frequency over time. Again, it is important to get the victim's perceptions, as well as those of the family and friends referred to earlier. Determining the severity of mistreatment is a crucial part of the assessment, since a victim's safety, and possibly his or her life, is at stake. This is a somewhat subjective assessment, and the worker, victim, and family and friends may have varying perceptions as to what harm has occurred already and what could possibly happen in the future. The worker needs to integrate these varying perceptions. Elements to consider are (1) the degree to which the victim, family, and friends minimize or exaggerate the consequences of mistreatment, (2) the extent to which harm has been observed by others, and (3) the degree to which the victim has required medical or police assistance because of mistreatment.

COGNITIVE STATUS

The intervention approach to be utilized is greatly influenced by the cognitive status of the victim. Determining cognitive status, therefore, is a key element of the assessment. To get a rough estimate of the cognitive abilities of a client, the worker should utilize an instrument, such as the Dementia Scale and/or Mini-Mental Status Exam (see Appendixes B and C). There are gradations of competence. Even if the victim is not sufficiently impaired as to require a guardian or conservator, there may be significant impairments impeding the victim's ability to self-preserve. For example, a worker should ascertain if the victim can conceptualize the multi-step planning required to escape an abusive episode, or if the victim possesses the cognitive ability to understand the risks and consequences of remaining in an abusive situation. Certainly, determining the degree of cognitive impairment can be much more complicated than simply administering the Dementia Scale or Mini-Mental Status Exam. If the worker suspects cognitive difficulty, a thorough neuropsychological evaluation should be performed by a qualified professional.

Often, living with considerable danger can result in depression. Before determining a victim to be impaired cognitively, it is important to rule out another underlying but reversible cause of dementia, such as depression. If a victim becomes hospitalized and is described by an accompanying caregiver as confused or demented, it is important for the health care provider to observe the victim's behavior in the hospital, away from the home, in order to assess accurately the victim's cognitive status. Is the older person confused in the hospital after appropriate care and proper nutrition have been provided? If there is a mismatch between the caregiver's history and observations in a controlled environment, further investigation is warranted.

HEALTH AND FUNCTIONAL STATUS

The health and functional status of the victim should also be carefully assessed, since the degree of independent functioning and care needs will influence case planning. This assessment will also help determine whether or not neglect is an element of the mistreatment, since neglect can occur only when the older person is dependent on someone else for assistance. Consider these questions when determining a victim's health and functional status: Is the victim mobile? Can the victim see? Hear? What is the extent of the impairment(s)? Is the victim on medications? If so, for what reason? What is the dosage prescribed? Does the victim have a special diet? Does the victim need assistance with activities of daily living? If so, what help is required and who provides it? Who is the victim's physician and how often is there follow-up?

ABUSER PROFILE

A comprehensive assessment should also seek to develop as clear a picture as possible of the abuser and the role he or she has in the elder's daily activities. Ask the following questions to gather information about the abuser: How is the victim related to the abuser? Does the abuser have a drug or alcohol problem? Is there a history of mental illness? Does the abuser provide care to the victim? If so, what types of care does this person provide? How many hours and what kinds of tasks does the care entail? Does the abuser live with the victim? If so, who is on the lease or deed? How frequent is the contact between the abuser and the victim? Is the abuser interested in talking with the worker making the assessment? Is the abuser interested in receiving help? (Please see Abusers section for further discussion.)

INTENT

In order to assess intent, the worker should ask the victim why he or she thinks the abuse is occurring, when the abuse started, and what circumstances usually surround abusive behaviors. If the victim is agreeable, it will help to clarify the situation by also asking these questions of nonabusing relatives, friends, and neighbors.

VICTIM AND COMMUNITY RESOURCES

As part of the assessment procedure, an evaluation of the victim's resources should be conducted. Eligibility for many services, including counseling, home care, and shelter, frequently depends on the victim's income and personal assets, as well as functional and health status. And the availability of nonabusing relatives, friends, and neighbors often determines the extent to what outside support is needed.

Usually, there is no one agency that can provide the full range of services needed. For example, it is unusual for one agency to provide medical assistance, shelter services, counseling, and court advocacy. A creative challenge for the worker is carefully to package existing community resources to fit a client's needs. This requires a careful evaluation of what the worker's own agency can provide and a full knowledge of what resources exist in the community. Often, workers feel inadequate or helpless when working with elder mistreatment victims, and because of this, refer the victims elsewhere for help before adequately assessing what services their own agencies can provide.

INTERVENTION HISTORY

The worker formulates intervention plans as the scope of the problem becomes clearer through the assessment process. Before finalizing a plan, the worker should find out what, if any, interventions were made in the past, what the outcomes were, and why the victim may be interested in help now. This can be ascertained by asking the victim and involved friends, relatives, and neighbors, and, with the victim's permission, agencies which may have been involved in the past.

Next, the worker should try to ascertain what the outcomes of past interventions were. If they were unsuccessful, why? This will help the worker better understand and avoid possible pitfalls when developing new assistance strategies. For example, a victim may not want to use the courts because in the past no protection from the abuser was provided after legal intervention was initiated. The elder mistreatment victim may have used the courts in the years before the battered women's movement had an impact on how the criminal justice system handles victim's rights. The worker would need to know this in order to explain why using the court system now may have a more positive outcome. Also, knowledge of successful past interventions is important because previous strategies which worked may prove to be useful again. In some mistreatment situations there is more than one abuser; for example, a woman could be mistreated by both her husband and her son. Perhaps she has used a strategy successfully against her husband, such as obtaining an Order of Protection, but has not attempted to obtain one against her son. The worker would want to find out what made the Order of Protection successful with the husband and ascertain if the same strategy could be applied to the son.

CATEGORIZING ABUSE

While there is no one prototypical elder mistreatment case or victim, it is possible to create general categories that help to narrow the field of intervention possibilities and guide the worker's approach to a specific case. There are two methods of categorizing victims that are not mutually exclusive and can be effectively used in conjunction with each other. Indeed, it is useful to consider how each case of mistreatment fits into both frameworks.

The first categorization was developed by the Legal Research and Services to the Elderly in Massachusetts and the National Paralegal Institute in California. Four classes of elder abuse victims were developed, each having "as their point of reference the client's *right* and *ability* to determine the system's response to his/her problems" (LRSE, 1981). These classes are:

(1) *competent, consenting client*: the client who appears to be mentally competent and who consents to assessment and assistance
(2) *competent, nonconsenting client*: the client who appears to be mentally competent and who may refuse assessment and does refuse assistance
(3) *incompetent client*: the client who (regardless of his or her degree of cooperation) appears to lack sufficient mental capacity to make informed decisions concerning his or her own care
(4) *emergency client*: the client who is in immediate danger of death or serious physical or mental harm, and who may or may not consent to help and may or may not be mentally competent

When a victim is identified or suspected, the worker first determines which of these categories applies. This determination will guide all future interventions. In this book, we are primarily concerned with three of the four categories: (1) competent, consenting, (2) competent, nonconsenting, and (3) competent, emergency clients.

The second categorization, to which we refer throughout the rest of the book, is called the Staircase Model (developed by Risa Breckman, Victim Services Agency's Elder Abuse Project, 1983), and is based primarily on the receptivity of victims to helping themselves. (See Figure 4.1.) The bottom of the staircase represents "life with mistreatment" and the top of the staircase represents "life without mistreatment." The staircase has three steps, or stages, representing the process of change: reluctance, recognition, and rebuilding. Intervention strategies are aimed at helping victims move toward the rebuilding stage. As part of the assessment, therefore, the worker should ascertain where the victim is on the Staircase Model. Service options that do not appeal to a victim in the reluctance stage are more likely to be favored by victims in the recognition and rebuilding stages. Note also that an individual victim can sometimes be in overlapping stages. For instance, a victim might be in the recognition stage regarding denial, and yet still be in the reluctance stage regarding isolation.

The following sections describe the different features of each of the three stages of this model.

Reluctance

In the reluctance stage, victims have a low self-acceptance level and tend to blame themselves for their abusive relative's problems. They have little tolerance for discussions about the possibility of making changes in their lives. To many of the victims in this stage, alternatives which directly address the abuse issue, for example, an Order of Protection, are of no interest because they have not yet framed the problem as one of mistreatment. Rather than ask for help for themselves, they are likely to ask instead for help for the abuser. Ironically, the more frequent and severe the mistreatment, often the stronger the belief by the victim that the abuser is in need of assistance.

As pointed out in Chapter 1, many abusers have serious psychiatric problems, or drug and alcohol addictions, so there is a good deal of validity in the reasoning that it is the abuser who needs help. The problem is that many abusers refuse to accept help, even when directed to do so by the courts. And, even if the abuser does recover from the psychiatric illness or substance abuse, there is no guarantee that the abusive pattern of behavior will end.

In many cases, victims in the reluctance stage already have extensive familiarity with alcohol, drug, and psychiatric treatment facilities and programs to which the abusers could be referred. Still, the victims conceptualize the problem as one of locating even better services for abusing relatives, and they fail to admit the significance of the mistreatment in their own lives.

These victims feel very uncomfortable about revealing anything which might portray their abusing relatives in a negative light. Often they feel ambivalent about reaching out for help at all, imagining this as a betrayal of trust. Indeed, many abusers will encourage these feelings of guilt by saying things such as: "*You* abuse me! I don't go around telling people our family problems. What kind of parent does that, anyway?"

Victims in this stage tend to be very isolated from friends and other family members. Visitors may have stopped coming to the house

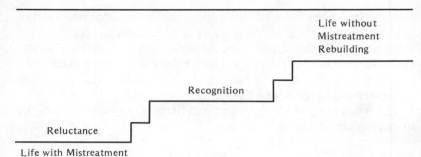

Reluctance Assessment	Recognition Assessment	Rebuilding Assessment
— Has not acknowledged the abuse.	— Recognition that problem is serious and complex, and that it can't be managed alone.	— Reshaping of identity. Seeking lifestyle alternatives.
— Tremendous denial, self-blame, low self-acceptance, ambivalence.	— Lessening of denial, self-blame. Still ambivalent. Self-acceptance high in some areas, low in others.	— Diminished self-blame. High self-acceptance.
— Extremely isolated.	— Wants to share with someone.	— Development of a support system.

Intervention	Intervention	Intervention

A. Provide emergency assistance.
 	
B. Give information on
  1. elder mistreatment:
    a. not alone;
    b. usually increases in incidence and severity.
  2. Options:
    a. counseling, e.g., individual, couple, family or group.*
    b. legal, e.g., Order of Protection, jail sentence for
	A. Provide emergency assistance.
	
	B. Explore options extensively, as listed in Reluctance.
	
	C. Provide services according to need and/or make appropriate referrals.
		A. Provide emergency assistance.
		
		B. Assist with adjustment to new housing, enforcement of Order of Protection, or other significant changes designed to stop mistreatment.
		
		C. Provide services according to need and/or make appropriate referrals.

(continued)

abuser, mandated
drug/alcohol and
educational pro-
grams for abuser.

c. financial services,
e.g., direct deposit,
representative
payee, Power-of-
Attorney.

d. housing alternatives,
e.g., moving, evict-
ing abuser, programs
offering help in the
home or with ADL.

e. lock replacement.

f. advocacy programs.

g. Adult Protective
Services.

3. accessing help:

a. give emergency
numbers;

b. review concrete
steps to follow if
conflict starts.

C. Implement a "keep in
touch" method, e.g.,
telephone reassurance.

D. Provide services according
to need and/or make
appropriate referrals.

*Couple and Family counseling is only indicated if abusive behavior has stopped.

Figure 4.1 Staircase Model: A Tool for Assessment and Case Management Planning
with Competent Victims of Elder Mistreatment (Created by Risa Breckman, Victim Services Agency, 1983)

because they feel uncomfortable or because the abusing relative refuses
access. Often the abusing relative monitors or screens phone calls. Some
victims may have close friends, but do not talk to these friends about
their family problems. They do not want outsiders to think badly about
their family, or the particular family member, so they keep the problem
to themselves. The end result is often that they feel separated and
isolated from even their dearest companions.

In addition, most elder mistreatment victims do not realize that many
people have similar problems. This fosters feelings of self-blame and

shame. The less contact the victim has with others, the more the contact with the abuser is valued. The more isolated the victim becomes, the less likely his or her perceptions of the problems at home are to be challenged or changed. It is a cruel irony that so many victims suffer their pain in silence, each thinking that he or she is alone and at fault.

Case Study: Reluctance

The following case example illustrates the reluctance stage. (Note that the same victim will be the focus of the case illustrations that follow depicting the recognition and rebuilding stages.)

A 63-year-old woman comes to the service center, having been referred there by a local senior center. She is looking for services for her 33-year-old son, who is living in her apartment and working as a taxi driver during his "good months." The son has a long history of psychiatric hospitalizations, and his mother thinks that what he really needs is to find a psychiatrist "who could cure him once and for all." Then, she imagines, he could get a regular job, find a girlfriend, get married, and live in a place of his own.

Upon further discussion, it becomes evident that her son has been prescribed medication for his illness. In a pattern that has been repeated, however, soon after leaving the hospital he stops taking the medication. A downward spiral of mood swings and aggressive behaviors inevitably follows. First, he becomes verbally aggressive, then he physically abuses his mother, for instance, by punching her in the chest.

The woman *blames herself* for her son's problems. Her sister told her once that she must have done something terribly wrong as a parent for her son to have turned out this way. She agrees: "I was so overprotective. I think that's why he has so many problems now."

The woman *denies* the seriousness of the problem, however. "It won't get worse; I'm not afraid of that." Yet, when describing the problem to the agency professional, it becomes clear that the mistreatment is escalating, in terms of both intensity and density. Another indication of *denial* is the fact that the woman does not understand why outsiders consistently focus attention on her safety needs, rather than on her son's psychiatric needs. She says to the worker, "I want help for my son, and everyone is trying to help me. I don't understand this." She also feels very *isolated*, reporting that, "I don't see my friends or family much anymore. Oh, I guess I see my sister some days, but for the most part, nobody wants to come over."

She expresses *low self-acceptance*: "I can't do anything right." When pressed to elaborate, she expresses that she thinks of herself as a "bad housekeeper, cook, and grocery shopper, as well as a lousy mother, wife, and sister."

Finally, the woman is uncomfortable talking about any of these problems and *ambivalent* about accepting help. She maintains that her son was "truly a good boy" and that perhaps she should never have come in and said anything at all.

Recognition

In the recognition stage, elder mistreatment victims begin to recognize that the problem is serious and complex, and that they can no longer manage alone. Victims become interested in talking about the mistreatment, in addition to talking about their abusing loved one's problems. They are more willing to come for counseling, join support groups, or talk for extended periods on the phone.

As part of this new stage, there is a lessening of denial and self-blame, and an increase in self-acceptance levels. There is also a decrease in feelings of ambivalence. Victims are genuinely interested in thinking about different ways of approaching the mistreatment problem, and they are open to new suggestions. Many feel, however, as though they are "caught between a rock and a hard place"—they are uncomfortable with the present status quo, but all available options seem equally or even more unpleasant.

Victims also attempt to decrease their isolation in this stage. Victims often make contact with friends and family whom they have not been in touch with for a while, and they are more open to meeting new people and trying new experiences. Some of the victims look into volunteer and employment options, or rejoin groups to which they used to belong. Some of these efforts are thwarted by abusers. Indeed, often victims in this stage fear retaliation by the abuser for trying to make contact with others. But the hallmark of this stage is an increased desire to talk with others, and an effort is made to do so.

Case Study: Recognition

The following continues the case example begun earlier, this time illustrating the recognition stage.

The victim tells her counselor that she has changed her view on seeking help for herself. There is now *less denial*. "Before I thought I should be able to handle this problem alone. Coming for help made me feel bad, made me feel helpless. I feel differently now."

She has *less self-blame* about her responsibility for her son's problems. "I don't feel totally responsible for his problems now. Although I made mistakes, I think I tried my hardest to raise him well."

She expresses a desire to meet regularly with a counselor and to talk with others going through similar experiences. In this way there is *less isolation*. "I think it would be nice to talk with someone regularly. Can we do that? And I would like to find out more about the support group. What do others do in my situation?"

The victim begins to reflect on the way she views herself outside of her role as mother. She recognizes that she has a poor self-image, and questions her need to be perfect, which reflects her *increased self-acceptance*. "When I am asked to write down the things in my life I have felt good about and the qualities in myself I like, it's a short list. Maybe it's because I always feel a need to be perfect and can't be. Nobody is."

She also begins to realize that she does not have to let her son live with her when he is discharged from the mental hospital. She still struggles with saying no to him, and cannot clearly envision herself doing so, but she is able to articulate the possibility, and therefore is *less ambivalent*. "My son begged me to take him home after he gets out of the mental hospital, but I told him he can't come home this time. I guess if he didn't like the halfway house and showed up on my doorstep, it would be awfully hard to turn him away. It probably wouldn't be good for either of us in the long run, but I'd let him in."

Rebuilding

In the rebuilding stage, elder abuse victims reshape their identity and actively seek lifestyle alternatives. They no longer think that they must be perfect in order to like themselves. They are willing to risk losing connection with an abusive family member; they have other people to rely on and no longer believe they are responsible for their family member's happiness.

Some victims in this stage still have contact with the abuser, but they use a wide range of options to keep themselves safe, including the police, courts, and temporary emergency shelters. One hallmark of this stage is that the victims no longer believe they must tolerate mistreatment in order to prove devotion to their abusing relatives.

Although the victim is in the rebuilding stage, the abusive relative may still try to mistreat, and might be successful as some abusers hound the victim, going to great lengths to discover their whereabouts if the victim has secretly relocated. Still, the distinguishing feature of this stage is that the victim does not compromise safety in order to maintain a connection with the abusive relative.

Case Study: Rebuilding

The following continues our case example, this time illustrating the rebuilding stage.

Withough denial or ambivalence, the victim now tells her counselor that she knows that she needs to find a new apartment and to keep the location a secret from her son. Although she does not let her son in when he is discharged from the mental hospital, he still comes around and harasses her. "I need to find a new apartment. A place where my son can't find me and hurt me. Kicking him out hasn't been the complete answer because he still comes around and haunts me. The truth is, I miss him. But I enjoy the time alone, just to relax and get to know myself better."

Demonstrating the *absence of self-blame*, she reflects much differently on her parenting role. "I have thought a great deal about how I raised him. There isn't one psychiatrist who can conclusively say what caused his mental illness. All these years I have blamed myself, thinking that I caused it by divorcing his father and then spoiling him. But that doesn't get me anywhere. I did my best and although I made mistakes, everyone does. Actually, I think I did rather well as a parent."

No longer isolated, she also reflects on what counseling has meant to her. "Counseling hasn't always been convenient for me. But it has helped me find the support I need and to ask others for support and to find new friends. Friends who don't have the same problems can't understand me fully, but its good to socialize because it puts my mind on other things and keeps me young."

She also reports a *state of self-acceptance* and is able to reflect on how her previous low self-acceptance made it difficult for her to help herself or even effectively help her son. "I am feeling good about myself now. I have been thinking that if people don't think about themselves first then they can't really have anything much to give to others. I want to think about myself more and I can't really help my son if I don't first help myself."

ABUSERS

In order to understand the extent of the abuse situation, it is necessary to not only assess the victim's needs and care status, but also that of the abuser. Many times, by understanding the abuser, and finding ways to treat his or her problems, the alleviation of the victim's suffering is also accomplished.

At one time or another, many professionals work with abusers. Protective service workers often interview abusers when responding to emergency calls, as do the police. Doctors, nurses, and social workers commonly interview abusers in hospitals, when they accompany their older relative for medical visits, and during home visits. At times, professionals are unaware that they are working with abusers. For example, it is common for abusers to enter drug treatment programs and remain undetected as people violent toward family members. Abusers with severe psychopathology are frequently institutionalized and not identified as people violent toward family members. Often they are returned home after discharge, without any consideration of the potential for recurrent elder mistreatment.

Workers have a range of thoughts and feelings about the abusers of elderly victims. The determining factor in the worker's response is usually the abuser's intent to harm. Workers are generally sympathetic when the mistreatment has occurred unintentionally. For example, people who abuse or neglect unintentionally may have assumed caregiving responsibilities and are incapable of providing adequate care, or have a mental disorder (e.g., dementia, mental retardation, substance addiction, and mental illness) contributing to the abusive or neglectful behavior. (Abusers unintentionally mistreating are not discussed further, as unintentional abuse and neglect are not the focus of this book.)

There is no guarantee that when a mental disorder is treated, the abusive behavior will stop. For example, an abuser no longer using drugs might continue to abuse out of a need to control. Similarly, there are those successfully treated for their mental illness who might continue to abuse, for the reasons outlined in the category *Abusers with malevolent motives*.

In situations in which an elderly person is harmed intentionally, most workers are outraged. It is our clinical impression that there are two categories of intentional abuse:

(1) *Abusers and neglectors with caregiving stress.* There is a small minority of caregivers who deliberately mistreat because they cannot cope with the demands of caregiving. The likelihood of their mistreating is not necessarily linked to the amount of care they provide, or to the amount of care their elderly relatives need. These tend to be people without a previous history of mistreatment and they are usually remorseful and shocked by their own behavior: the daughter responsible for the 24-hour care of her father with Alzheimer's who threw a dish at him after his afternoon feeding took two hours, or the wife of a man with a recent leg amputation who screams at him mercilessly to move faster while helping him to the bathroom.

(2) *Abusers with malevolent motives.* These are people who mistreat out of greed, a sense of powerlessness, and an inability to tolerate frustration. Examples include the son of a Parkinson's disease patient who refuses to purchase necessary services, attempting to preserve financial resources for his inheritance; a grandson who was recently divorced and fired from his job and, out of his own self-hatred, sexually assaults his grandmother; a wife who, angry at her husband for not wanting to participate at a family function, hits him. These abusers may or may not deliver care, be

drug and/or alcohol dependent, or have a mental disorder. If they do use alcohol or drugs, this habit is often used to excuse the abusive behavior, for example, "I didn't mean to hurt you, Mom. I was just so drunk!"

ASSESSMENT OF THE ABUSER

The following factors should be considered when assessing an abuser's service needs before developing an intervention plan.

(1) *Type of abuser:* Which abuser category fits this abuser? What motivated the mistreatment? Was the mistreatment intentional or unintentional? What proof exists?

(2) *Type of mistreatment:* What mistreatment has occurred (physical, psychological, financial, neglect)?

(3) *Severity and duration of mistreatment:* What damage has resulted from the mistreatment? How has this affected the victim? How has this affected the abuser's life? Over what period of time has the mistreatment occurred? Were there any intervals of time when mistreatment did not occur?

(4) *Abuser acknowledgment of behavior and willingness to accept help:* Has the abuser admitted any wrongdoing? Does the abuser minimize the seriousness of his or her actions? Does the abuser see a connection between his or her behavior and resulting harm? Does the abuser blame somebody else for problems (e.g., the victim, other household member)? Does the abuser blame problems alcohol, loss of a job, a divorce, the death of a loved one? Does the abuser want help?

(5) *Past and present interventions with the abuser:* What interventions have been tried before with the abuser? What helped, and why? What didn't help and why? Does the abuser have a criminal record? If so, for what and when did the crime(s) occur? Does this record have any bearing on intervention plans? Is the abuser currently being assisted regarding the mistreatment problems?

(6) *Safety risk to professional in helping abuser:* Is the professional's safety compromised by helping the abuser? Is the abuse only directed to family and not outsiders? Does the worker's organization have a safety policy? Is it adequate? Will there be a safety issue for other workers engaged in the intervention plan (e.g., home attendants)?

Other issues to consider when assessing an abuser's service needs are the abuser's physical, mental, and functional status; the victim's desire to involve the abusing relative; organizational and professional responsibilities and capabilities; professional, victim, and family observations of the abuser; the availability of community resources/informal network; financial resources; and transportation.

INTERVENTIONS WITH ABUSERS

There are many intervention options for abusers. These are listed below. This list is divided into five general categories. (See Table 4.1.) Which services are provided to an abuser depends on the configuration of assessment factors.

Also, specific interventions are commonly used for the different types of abusers. (See Table 4.2.) As mentioned previously, not all of these services are available in every community, nor does every abuser accept help voluntarily.

Not all victims remain passive when mistreated. Some victims defend themselves by using physical force. Indeed, there are cases in which the victims have seriously harmed or killed their abusers. Victims may be brought into the criminal justice system as defendants. In these cases, professionals might mistakenly consider the victims to be abusers. Rather, these victims are in need of tremendous advocacy, support, counseling, and good legal representation, much the same as when younger battered women harm or kill their abusive husbands.

TABLE 4.1
Intervention Options for the Abuser

Counseling & Treatment	Respite & Assistance	Education	Law Enforcement & Courts	Living Arrangements
individual, couple, family, group	help in the home, such as home attendant, meals on wheels, housekeeper, respite workers	education on caregiving, short- and long-term effects of mistreatment, programs available	police, court-mandated programs, incarceration	other living arrangement for abuser, e.g., nursing home, group home, separate apartment, house, or with friends or family
support group for caregivers	concrete or emotional support from informal network, e.g., friends, relatives	educational groups modeled after those developed for younger batterers, to teach alternatives to violence	court-mandated educational groups modeled after those developed for younger batterers, to teach alternatives to violence	limit or cease contact with elder
psychiatric treatment and medical assessment, or institutionalization			limit or cease contact with elder	
drug and alcohol treatment programs, in-patient or out-patient				
educational groups modeled after those developed for younger batterers, to teach alternatives to violence				
vocational counseling and job placement programs				

TABLE 4.2
Interventions with Abusers by Abuser Category

Abusers and Neglectors with Caregiving Stress	Abusers with Malevolent Motives
individual, couple or family counseling	individual counseling, drug and alcohol treatment programs, in-patient or out-patient
support group for caregivers	educational groups modeled after those developed for younger batterers, to teach alternatives to violence
education on caregiving, short- and long-term effects of mistreatment and programs available	vocational counseling and placement
programs offering caregiver respite, such as help in the home, meals-on-wheels, respite workers	education on community resources and the short- and long-term effects of mistreatment
obtain concrete and emotional support from informal network, e.g., friends, relatives	police, court orders, and mandated programs, incarceration
	limit or cease contact with the abuser
	other living arrangements for abusers, e.g., nursing home, group home, separate apartment, house, or with friends or family

Chapter 5

INTERVENTION

In this chapter, we will describe intervention methods to use when helping competent elder mistreatment victims, using the Staircase Model (Figure 1) as a framework for discussion.

RELUCTANCE

In this stage, intervention strategies are targeted at breaking through the victim's denial and decreasing feelings of isolation, guilt, and self-blame. At the same time efforts are directed at increasing the victim's feelings of self-acceptance and providing the victim with options in responding appropriately to emergencies.

Workers often express feelings of helplessness when a victim of elder mistreatment refuses assistance. They know that the victim will most likely suffer more pain and harm without their help. And they acknowledge that competent elders have the right to make their own decisions, just as is the case for younger adults, even if those decisions leave them in a precarious situation.

For example, many younger battered women choose to remain in violent households. For many of these women, there are economic and social constraints they feel prohibit them from leaving. Others, however, choose to remain with violent husbands because of an emotional attachment. The same is often true with elder mistreatment victims. For many, there is a strong emotional attachment to the abuser that prohibits them from making life-style changes.

Workers need support when working with elder mistreatment victims who refuse assistance. The feelings of helplessness and inadequacy can be powerful, making it is necessary to receive supervision and feedback from colleagues.

General principles to follow when assisting a suspected victim of elder mistreatment or someone who has admitted to being victimized are:

Decrease isolation. If someone is a suspected victim of elder mistreatment, he or she should be provided with information about the problem. Victims cannot adequately help themselves if they do not have accurate information about mistreatment. If the older person has not disclosed the mistreatment directly, the victim probably has strong feelings of shame about the problem or has denied the seriousness of the situation. Or, if the suspicion is unconfirmed by physical and behavioral symptoms, it may well be that the person is not denying a problem— rather, he or she may not have been abused or neglected. In many cases the worker may not have enough time or contact with the older person to make a definitive assessment. Providing information about elder mistreatment can do no harm, whether or not the person is being mistreated.

The issue should be raised in a matter-of-fact way. The worker should explain that he or she wants to talk about a serious problem that affects thousands of older people each year. The worker can also say that it is the organization's policy to talk with all older people about the problem of elder mistreatment, in the same way workers routinely discuss drug or alcohol use. By making the discussion routine, the issue is destigmatized.

It will help to explain that recent research suggests that each year approximately one million older Americans suffer physical, psychological, or financial abuse at the hands of relatives. Workers should ask older clients if this is a problem which relates to them or someone they know. Observe the potential victim carefully during this discussion and listen to everything they have to say. If the older person discusses the issue of mistreatment frankly, as if talking about any other social problem, this is a strong indication that elder mistreatment is not a personal problem. Other individuals may say that a neighbor or friend is being mistreated and want information on how to help. This may be a genuine response, and clear information on how to help their friend should be provided. On the other hand, such a response might be a way for the person to get information for him- or herself without having to disclose the mistreatment. Victims might avert their eyes, change the subject, or ask directly, "Why are you telling me this?" Other victims might say that it is interesting information, yet, because of their own denial, will not relate the information to themselves. Nonetheless, it might be the first time they have heard that they are not alone in their pain, and they will remember it.

This strategy allows the worker to further educate possible victims about elder mistreatment. The next step is to inform the older person that mistreatment tends to increase in frequency and severity over time. Since victims in the reluctance stage deny that abuse exists at all, this assertion may sound strange to them. But because victims in this stage usually continue to live with or have extensive contact with the abuser, it is crucial information to impart.

Decrease guilt, shame, and self-blame. Victims in the reluctance stage frequently have feelings of self-blame, shame, and guilt. These and other debilitating feelings, according to cognitive therapy theorists, are caused by irrational thoughts or "magical thinking" (Ellis, 1973, p. 6). The hallmarks of these irrational thoughts are the words *should, ought,* and *must.* Behind these words is the notion that life, in general, is supposed to treat us only favorably, that other people are supposed to always treat us well, and that, as individuals, we are not supposed to make mistakes.

An example of this kind of thinking is, "I must think of my son's welfare before my own, otherwise I am not a good parent." Unfortunately, many victims of elder mistreatment adopt this type of thinking. When they act in their own self-interest, for example, call the police on an abusive relative, they soon feel tremendous guilt when they think of the family member being arrested.

When counseling victims, workers can help them change their guilt-inducing thoughts to other, more positive thoughts that do not result in guilt feelings. This can be accomplished by helping the victim rethink the concept of what constitutes a "good" parent, and to help the victim include in the definition behaviors that set limits on destructive behavior. In this way, the worker is helping to reframe actions that appear to be only serving the victim's best interest, such as the action of calling the police, as something that actually is helpful for the abuser, too. The worker can explain that it is not helpful for the abusive son, daughter, or spouse when that person is permitted to act on angry feelings. For example, a physically abusive son could seriously injure or kill his mother, and could be sentenced to jail for assault or homicide.

Another way of helping a victim change a guilt-inducing thought is by working toward changing the word *must.* The *must* in the sentence, "I must think of my son's welfare before my own" is an absolute, with no evidence supporting it. There are many parents who do not sacrifice their own safety in order to prove they are "good" parents. Workers can help victims challenge their own thinking by helping them realize that there are many other ways to view parenting, and by giving themselves an absolute they are putting themselves in a dangerous bind.

Elder mistreatment victims tell themselves, "I should have realized a long time ago that she had a drug problem. I didn't help her then and I should do something about it now." Implicit in a statement like this is, "I am responsible. I was not a good parent. It's my fault and I have to undo what I did." The *shoulds* in the statement induce tremendous guilt and self-blame. In addition, these statements illustrate how little forgiveness the victims have for themselves.

Shame is another emotion with which victims are confronted. Victims have a tremendous concern for what others would think of them if they knew of the mistreatment. They usually think, "Others will look down on me if they know. They will think I've done something wrong. I don't want them to think badly of me."

By using cognitive therapeutic techniques, workers can help victims analyze the folly of this thinking. First, there is no evidence to support the supposition that everyone will think poorly of them. The worker is an important example of someone not judging the victim negatively. Also, the victim is thinking that he or she is at fault, that the problem is too hideous to talk about, and that nobody else has these problems. The victim thinks this is why others will think poorly of him or her if they know. Counselors need to make sure that they do not passively or actively agree with these thoughts. Through counseling, whether in group or individual sessions, victims learn that only by sharing of themselves can they receive support and that this reward is worth the risk of rejection.

One way victim support groups help to ease some of the feelings of shame is by giving victims a chance to practice talking about the victimization with others. By having to cope with a range of positive and negative feedback from group members, they learn that their happiness is not determined by what others think of them. There are also numerous "shame-attacking" exercises that can be applied to work with victims of elder mistreatment (Walen, DiGiuseppe, & Wessler, 1980, pp. 225-228).

Educate about options. Suspected victims need to be told that there are alternatives to abusive situations. They need information concerning access to the police, courts, the criminal justice system and the availability of temporary safe places to stay. (There are other options to consider as well. See Figure 4.1 for additional listing.) The worker should assist the victim in determining which family and friends they can rely on for support and to help in emergencies.

Victims in the reluctance stage generally respond to this information in one of two ways. Some listen intently to what is being said, but, because of their denial, do not understand the reason why they are being told about mistreatment. Others respond by stating that they do not need or want to talk about it. But, no matter how the suspected victim responds, it is imperative that he or she have the information. One approach workers may take is to say that it is the agency policy to provide such information to all seniors, and, in such cases, it is advisable to have a special data or resource sheet that can be presented to the older person, which they can read at home.

Help with emergencies. Many victims in the reluctance stage call the police during an abusive episode and at times need emergency medical assistance. Once help is received, these victims often deny that there is any trouble at home. After responding appropriately to the emergency, workers have the opportunity to talk with suspected victims about their present situation and the possibility of future problems. Suspected victims should be questioned about tense situations at home. What are those situations like? What are the signs that tension is building and how do they handle this? Do they know how to access the police or other emergency help? Do they have alternate places to stay if necessary? Will they have access to money in an emergency?

When asked these questions, some people respond indignantly or with confusion. This could mean that the suspicion of abuse is incorrect. But asking these tough questions is not harmful and, in fact, for those people who are truly victims, they may be life-saving. The suspected victim should be given referral numbers to call in an emergency, including any appropriate 24-hour victim hot line and crisis intervention numbers.

Keep in touch. Victims in the reluctance stage, because of their denial, tend to minimize the seriousness of their situation. To address the victim denial directly, workers should arrange a "keep-in-touch" method with them. The worker should ask the victim to call once a week so he or she can know if the problems at home have continued. If this is not acceptable, perhaps the worker could send a letter. If the victim agrees to call, ask what the back-up plan should be if the arranged contact is not made. The worker might suggest that he or she will call the victim in this case. If the victim agrees, a decision must be made concerning what the worker should say in the event the victim does not answer the phone. This is necessary because victims often do not want family members to know they have established outside contact. For example, the worker could leave an agreed-upon message that would alert the victim of the call. The idea is to come up with a "keep-in-touch" method that the victim finds acceptable.

During the follow-up call or contact, the worker should ask the victim if he or she had a safe week. This question serves to remind the victim that the worker is not convinced that all is well at home. If the older person asks why the worker is concerned about his or her safety, the worker should reiterate that many older people are hurt by relatives and that he or she thought this might be happening at the client's home. If the older person says all is fine, the worker should not belabor the point. Instead, the worker should talk with the victim about what occurred during the past week, assessing by this means the degree of contact with others, opportunities for stimulation, or possible health and home care needs. The worker can use this information as a springboard for further discussion regarding isolation, safety, or other mistreatment-related issues.

As discussed earlier, isolation is an important risk factor of mistreatment. The worker should try asking the person if he or she is satisfied with the number of friends and the quality of the contact. If the older person acknowledges displeasure, ways of meeting new people or contacting old friends can be discussed, such as developing outside interests and hobbies, finding volunteer work, or possible employment. Workers should bear in mind that the victim might be prevented from having contact with outsiders by the abuser and may be hesitant to confide this fact. Also, some victims may be willing to meet new people provided they are accompanied by the worker on the first visit to the activity, senior center, or whatever.

During each follow-up phone call or visit, this process should be repeated, thereby working to overcome the victim's denial. If an abusive episode occurs, it will be easier for the victim to discuss it, since it will already have been made clear that the worker is willing to and interested in talking about such matters. Obviously, follow-up with suspected victims is a time-consuming process. Some elder mistreatment programs are able to train and recruit volunteers to provide this service. A "friendly" visiting program might agree to have volunteers do follow-up with victims. Properly trained student interns can be ideal for this important work.

RECOGNITION AND REBUILDING

Much of the intervention strategies begun in the reluctance stage are continued in the recognition stage. The goals of intervention remain to increase the victim's self-acceptance, lessen isolation and self-blame, and plan for and respond to emergencies. The most significant difference between the two stages is the acknowledgment on the victim's part of the mistreatment. Since ambivalence and denial is considerably less than it was in reluctance, services and strategies that were previously unacceptable to victims are now viable options.

Victims in the rebuilding stage actively pursue strategies that lead them toward a life without mistreatment. There is no longer denial about the mistreatment or ambivalence about seeking help. There are no feelings of guilt or self-blame, and the victim is no longer isolated. Much of the work in this stage consists of responding to emergencies and providing advocacy. This often means helping to obtain new housing or helping to get the police to respond appropriately to an Order of Protection. In the rebuilding stage, when the mistreatment continues, it is because the abusers continue to hound the victims and the systems fail to respond appropriately, not because of victim ambivalence.

Sometimes victims move in a descending direction on the staircase. For example, a victim may have tremendous denial for months and then finally acknowledge that his or her abuse situation is as serious as the abuser's alcohol problem. Then, after joining a support group for several months, the victim goes back to denying that the abuse is a problem and drops out of the group. This often frustrates workers, who begin to feel their past efforts were futile. But the cognitive and behavioral changes the victim has made are not lost. For the victim who denies the abuse again after having recognized its presence, the denial is not as powerful as it once was. What has been learned is remembered: Where to turn for help, what options exist, information on the pattern of family mistreatment. Breaking through the denial the second time is usually not as difficult as it was at first.

ISSUES FOR HOME
HEALTH PROFESSIONALS

Many older people require assistance with activities of daily living and there are many others who need the care of a skilled nurse or professional caregiver, such as a home attendant, home health aide, or visiting nurse. Because these people provide services within the home in which the older person resides, they are often the first to observe signs or symptoms of elder mistreatment.

For instance, they might notice changes in the victim's eating and sleeping patterns or changes in moods. If they are responsible for bathing the older person, they might see marks on the body that would not be visible when the person is dressed. They might also witness verbal aggression by a relative toward the older person and witness the victim's response. (In some cases, a relative may be verbally aggressive and the older person is not bothered by this; for other people, the verbal aggression leaves the older person feeling inadequate, worthless, and helpless.)

Some home care workers report fearing for their own safety. There have been circumstances in which the professional was threatened or assaulted. Certainly, there are homes in which agencies refuse to place professionals because of past threats or attacks against workers by the abusing relatives. There are also times when the abuser refuses the worker entry into the home. Knowing that the older person depends on them for care and then being denied access fills most workers with a sense of danger and outrage.

Suspecting mistreatment, a worker might try to talk with the older person about the situation. It is important for the worker to speak with his or her supervisor about the suspicions or actual incidents, so that responsibility for developing an intervention plan is shared. Also, it is important for the worker to discuss his or her own safety concerns, and to try to build in safeguards.

Case Study

The following example illustrates some signs of mistreatment that might be seen in the home and the difficult emergency decisions home health professionals might have to make in response to abusive overtures.

Ms. Butler was hired several weeks ago by the city to help Mrs. Lisner with activities of daily living while she recovered from a hip injury. Ms. Butler arrived every weekday at 8:00 a.m. and left at 5:00 p.m. Mrs. Lisner's daughter came three times a week to do the shopping, cleaning, and cooking. Mrs. Butler could feel the hostility between Mrs. Lisner and her daughter. It seemed that every interaction ended in an argument. The daughter would often storm out of the house, and Mrs. Lisner would just want to sleep, often not eating dinner, then not wanting to eat the next day, either.

After one particular argument, instead of leaving, the daughter demanded that Ms. Butler leave the house. Mrs. Lisner held her hand and told her to stay. Ms. Butler asserted that she would not leave her post, and the daughter stormed out of the house, leaving her mother weeping in bed. Ms. Butler quickly called her supervisor to get advice.

GUIDELINES FOR HOME
HEALTH PROFESSIONALS

Seek help from supervisor if abuse is suspected or witnessed. This should include a discussion of concerns about personal safety and information concerning any laws that govern the worker's handling of the situation. In addition, there should be guidance in determining a solid assessment and intervention plan and the availability of community resources. All professionals need feedback and support when working with abuse cases. Hopefully, staff supervisors can provide assistance. If not, cases can be discussed with colleagues or in staff conferences. The worker should continue to consult with colleagues and ask questions until she or he is satisfied with the information needed to help the victim.

Exercise caution. Home health professionals have reported many difficult and precarious situations—from an abuser banging on the door to active threats and actual violence. If there is an immediate danger, call the police. Workers should trust their instincts. Do not worry about being an alarmist. If a worker believes a home is a violent place and feels threatened, the worker should not enter until a safety plan is devised that provides security and comfort, for example, sending two workers to the home or using a beeper "check-in" system. It might be that the home situation is just too potentially dangerous to work in. A worker has a right to his or her personal safety.

Learn about reporting laws. Because workers visit households where there is elder mistreatment, it is imperative that they be familiar with local state reporting laws. Most states have laws requiring health professionals to report elder abuse and neglect. If elder mistreatment is suspected and state laws mandate reporting, the state will investigate. The state investigator will probably want to talk with the worker concerning her or his suspicions in order to assess the situation accurately. Most state reporting laws provide immunity from suits to those reporting the abuse.

Learn about community resources. Workers feel much more comfortable talking with older people about mistreatment if they are knowledgeable about the availability of local resources. The following services are commonly utilized by victims of mistreatment. Compile resource lists surveying these types of services: Adult Protective Services; emergency shelters and safe home projects; lock replacement and repair services; 24-hour hot line, crisis intervention, and counseling services; and legal assistance and court advocacy. In most localities there are gaps in services for victims of elder mistreatment. Fortunately, communities across the country are developing coalitions to address service needs and other issues pertaining to mistreatment.

SECONDARY VICTIMS

Sometimes the person calling for help is a neighbor, friend, or relative of the victim. Since these people are affected in some way by the mistreatment, they are called "secondary victims." In fact, secondary victims are more likely to report mistreatment situations than are doctors, nurses, and social workers (Alliance/Elder Abuse Project, 1983). Sometimes helping the victim requires responding to the calls made by neighbors, friends, and relatives. The following discussion outlines for workers the concerns of secondary victims and how to respond.

NEIGHBORS

When neighbors seek help for a victim, they have usually overheard domestic disturbances or noticed something unusual. If the victim resides in an apartment building, those neighbors with adjoining walls may hear arguments, pounding on walls, or even physical violence. They may see the victim wandering the hallway with injuries. They may hear the abuser banging on the door trying to gain access to the apartment. If there is a door attendant, he or she may be concerned that the older person has not been seen for a few days. In the suburbs and rural areas, mistreatment situations may be less apparent. However, neighbors might still notice a problem. Perhaps they haven't seen the older person outside for awhile. Or maybe they realize that the older person is unusually nervous, or they have seen bruises or other injuries.

Some neighbors reach out because they are deeply concerned for the victim's welfare. Others just want the disruptions to stop. Such neighbors might try to get the victim or the victim's family evicted from an apartment because the quality of life in the building is being disrupted.

Some neighbors report that when they approach the victim, the older person denies there is anything wrong. It is important to remember that many victims in the reluctance stage hide their pain in silence, out of shame or guilt; those in other stages may remain silent for fear of retaliation. Additionally, the older person may fear the eventual outcome should the outside world become involved. For example, the victim might think a neighbor will have the abuser arrested or tell nonabusing family members to have them placed into a nursing home.

The following example illustrates the way some neighbors are affected by and respond to elder mistreatment.

About once a month Sara's son would bang on her apartment door late at night, forcefully demanding entrance. Then, after 15 minutes of this, she would open her door and let him in. One particular neighbor was very upset by this repeated disturbance. On several occasions he heard the son screaming obscenities and demanding money. One afternoon the neighbor finally inquired about the incidents. He asked the woman if she wanted help. Sara averted her eyes and said that she was all right. Exasperated, the neighbor called the Department for the Aging to find out what could be done for her.

RELATIVES

Just as with neighbors, relatives often witness the consequences of the mistreatment victims suffer, such as deteriorating health, changes in mood, injuries, lowering of self-acceptance levels, and denial. Also, they may be concerned for the abuser. If the abuser has a drug or alcohol problem, often the relatives may confront him or her about this. If there has been a history of chronic mental illness, relatives may try to have the abuser hospitalized or prevent a discharge back into the older person's home. Or, after a violent episode, sometimes the victim may go to live with another relative.

These intervention attempts might not be successful. The older person might accept the abuser back after discharge from a psychiatric institution, or the abuser might not remain with a drug or alcohol rehabilitation program.

Family members often reach out to clergy, doctors, social workers, or the police, with the hope that an outsider will be more successful at stopping the abuse than they were. By the time nonabusing family members ask for help, they are often worn out from dealing with repeated episodes of mistreatment. Workers need to remember this, give the family members credit for their concern and prior efforts, and avoid judging family members harshly for not doing more.

The following example illustrates the questions relatives might ask when reaching out for help for the victim.

Case Illustration

A social worker was asked by a radio station to talk on a "call-in" show. A teenage listener phoned the show seeking advice on how to help her grandmother. She explained that an older grandson was living with the grandmother. He had a drinking problem and hadn't held a steady job for many years. He didn't help with the rent or the grocery bills. The family knew he beat her because they'd seen bruises. But the grandmother wouldn't kick him out. The young girl said that it had reached the point where some family members wouldn't even go to the house to visit. The question to the social worker was: How can the family get him out of the house?

FRIENDS

Sometimes it is a friend of the victim who seeks help. Perhaps the victim has confided to the friend that there are problems at home. Or maybe the friend noticed signs that something was wrong, such as a change in mood, evidence of bruises, a reluctance to invite guests over, or maybe an inability to talk on the phone without disruption. (This is not to imply that all friends believe the victim when he or she says there is abuse at home. Some victims report that friends and relatives are incredulous because they simply cannot believe that the person named as abusive could behave in such a way.)

The following example illustrates the way in which friends of victims might reach out for help.

A social worker conducted a workshop on elder abuse at a local senior center. When she completed her presentation, three seniors approached her. They said there was a 72-year-old man at the center who was being abused by his 15-year-old grandniece. She had broken his arm once and always wanted money for new clothes and records. The social worker said that she would speak with the gentleman if he wanted to talk with her. The three walked off together, and soon after returned with the victim.

Secondary victims may become impatient if the victim does not take a firm stand against the abuser. For example, if a friend of a victim suggests that the victim throw her abusive daughter out of the house, she or he might become frustrated when the victim worries about the daughter not having a place to live if she should do so. Sometimes, in their frustration, secondary victims begin to withdraw from the victim and the abusive situation. It is not uncommon for them to visit and call less often, which increases the isolation of the victim. As a result, the victim might receive fewer invitations to attend family events or might begin to decline invitations, feeling unwelcome or judged.

GUIDELINES FOR HELPING
SECONDARY VICTIMS

Inform secondary victims of what to do in an emergency. When counseling secondary victims, workers should inform them that if they hear or see a domestic dispute in progress, not to risk serious injury by intervening, but immediately call the police. When calling they should state that it is an emergency situation and give the address where the dispute is taking place. After the mistreatment is reported, they should watch for the police and, if they do not arrive promptly, call again.

Provide information about investigations. In most states, the concerned party can call Adult Protective Services (APS) to have the abuse situation investigated. Workers should explain to the secondary victim that if the investigator determines the primary victim to be competent and desires to remain in the environment, then the victim has a right to have this preference respected. If the victim is deemed incompetent, APS can intervene against the person's stated preference, hopefully opting for the least restrictive alternative. In some cases, APS can offer a range of services to the victim and the family. The number for APS can usually be found by dialing "information," through the police, or through the local Department for the Aging or the State Department of Social Services. Workers should inform the secondary victim that cooperating with APS staff will help facilitate a more accurate investigation.

Be aware, however, that many secondary victims will want to call in a report anonymously for a variety of reasons, including fear of retaliation by the abuser or fear of losing the victim's friendship and trust. Or, having already informed an agency or professional of the abusive situation, the caller may not want to proceed further. The secondary victim should be informed if local state law provides for immunity from civil and criminal liability for reporting mistreatment and if the law allows anonymous reports. If the worker can get the name, phone number, and address of the suspected victim, he or she might be able to help the victim directly, depending on the flexibility and policy of the agency or organization. In any event, thank secondary victims for their concern and let them know that they can call in the future, if needed.

Assess the situation and educate about abuse. Workers should try to ascertain from the secondary victim where the primary victim is on the Staircase Model. Inquire about what interventions have been made in the past, what worked, what did not work, and why. Also, try to determine the intensity of the mistreatment. Find out what types of abuses are occurring. Explain that victims go through stages in achieving a life without mistreatment and then explain to the secondary victim what thoughts, feelings, and behaviors they might expect from the victim they are calling about.

Encourage active listening and nonjudgmental concern. Secondary victims might try to talk with the victim privately to let the older person know they are concerned about his or her well-being. Encourage the secondary victims to let the primary victim know that it is not necessary to accept being harmed in order to be a good mother, father, grandparent, or spouse. The secondary victim should avoid being judgmental of the abuser, since this may alienate the victim. Help friends, relatives, and neighbors make statements to the victim such as, "Your son's (daughter's, niece's, etc.) behavior is bad and unacceptable," rather than, "Your son (daughter, niece, etc.) is bad and unacceptable." Also, they should stress to the victim that the violence probably will continue and get worse over time without intervention.

Encourage availability to help. Give the secondary victim specific tasks to work on with the victim that correspond to the appropriate stage on the Staircase Model. The secondary victim might offer a safe place to stay or offer to accompany the victim to court or to housing and doctor appointments. They might try to help the victim become involved in activities outside the home, for example, working, volunteering, joining a chorus, a book club, or a senior center, to decrease isolation. It is only when other significant contacts are developed that most victims feel ready to risk changing their relationship with the abuser.

Encourage patience. Workers should explain to secondary victims that family mistreatment situations develop slowly and usually are not resolved quickly. Ask the secondary victims if they think the primary victim has a right to make his or her own decision about what to do. Discuss their response, clarifying, if necessary, the fact that competent old people have the right to determine their own life-style, even if that means living with mistreatment.

Give referrals. Secondary victims need to know what services are available for the victim. In some instances, relatives, neighbors, and friends seek counseling for themselves as the psychological pain and pressure created by the mistreatment may be great. It is helpful for secondary victims to know that seeking counseling is something many people in their situation do and to offer help in providing referrals.

Chapter 6

INTERDISCIPLINARY PERSPECTIVES ON ELDER MISTREATMENT

In trying to achieve a life without mistreatment, victims interact with many systems and bureaucracies (e.g., mental health, criminal justice, social service, and health care systems). In order to serve clients properly, it is necessary for a professional working in one of these systems to know what the other systems offer victims of elder mistreatment, and how to access them. Also, it is often necessary for professionals from different disciplines to work together when detecting, assessing, and intervening in elder abuse situations, creating formal or informal "geriatric teams."

A geriatric team is formed when two or more people from different disciplines work together to assist a client with his or her health, functional status, and quality of life needs. Why form a geriatric team when working with victims of elder mistreatment? Often the issues are so complex that the victim requires more than one professional's knowledge and expertise.

In some settings, working within teams is common place. For example, in hospitals where there are either geriatric in-patient or out-patient units, usually a team consisting of a doctor, a nurse, and a social worker has been incorporated into the health care delivery structure. While the team consisting of a doctor, a nurse, and a social worker is perhaps the most common configuration, teams need not be limited to these professions. The idea is to form a team with representation from the necessary professions to maximize a client's care: The makeup of the team may change from client to client.

Most professionals work in settings that do not have formal geriatric teams. For these professionals, it is necessary to form informal teams by developing consultative relationships with professionals from other disciplines who are available to assist with elder mistreatment cases.

Leadership of the team is not relegated to any particular discipline. Rather, it is often determined by which professional is most familiar with the client or will have the most contact with the client over time.

Developing an effective, functional team is not always an easy task. Yet there are great benefits in pursuing successful team development, since each discipline offers a unique perspective into the understanding of client problems and the analyzing of possible solutions. The roles and responsibilities for each team member, based on client need, should be determined by the team. In this way, the entire care needs of a client are discussed and evaluated, and the responsibilities of care are shared.

Most of the time, when professionals are assigned to work on a team or volunteer to consult with one, there is a spirit of cooperation and the knowledge shared by one complements the others. There may also be conflicts among team members. For example, the team internist may think a victim competent, whereas the consulting psychiatrist may think the victim cognitively impaired. The team needs to appreciate and use the conflict constructively. For example, rather than sit in disagreement, the internist and psychiatrist may see this as an area that needs further assessment and agree to request a more thorough neuropsychological evaluation. One hallmark of successful team functioning is when conflict is acknowledged and discussed and the members can reach consensus on how best to proceed.

In this chapter, we present three different elder mistreatment case scenarios. The authors requested six professionals, each recognized for her or his knowledge in elder mistreatment, briefly to discuss possible detection, assessment, and intervention approaches for the cases. These professionals represent four disciplines: social work, law, nursing, and medicine. Two professionals from different disciplines responded independently to each case study presented in this chapter. The responses, therefore, are not "team" responses, that is, the professionals did not collaborate with each other to develop a unified response. Each respondent analyzed the roles and responsibilities of their own profession. At the end of each case study, there is a list of study questions to trigger further discussion. The cases and the accompanying study questions can also be used for training.

DELIA BUCK—CASE STUDY

Mrs. Delia Buck is an 87-year-old widow who lives alone in a two-bedroom apartment. Although she never had children, Mrs. Buck always considered her niece, Cynthia Philips, as her own daughter. She and her husband paid for Cynthia's college education and her wedding. (Unhappily, the marriage ended in divorce.) Indeed, Cynthia is Mrs. Buck's only living relative.

After Mr. Buck died three years earlier, Mrs. Buck was provided for by a $250,000 insurance policy. Initially, Cynthia visited her aunt often and helped her with financial affairs. After these financial affairs had been taken care of, Cynthia began to visit less frequently, usually once a month. She also kept in touch with occasional phone calls. Mrs. Buck was saddened by this development, but she has been reluctant to confront her niece. She confided in her neighbor and closest friend, Mrs. Apple, that "my niece has given so much of her time already. She has her own life to live, you know. She can't keep worrying about me."

Mrs. Buck functioned well until her eighty-fifth year, when she underwent bowel surgery for colon cancer that required a colostomy. Although unhappy with the change in her health, Mrs. Buck recovered from the surgery and was able to maintain her apartment, shop, cook meals, and take the appropriate measures for good colostomy care.

Since her discharge from the hospital, Mrs. Buck's progress has been monitored by a visiting nurse. As the situation improved, the visits became less frequent, and the nurse visited Mrs. Buck's home only every six months. Mrs. Buck looked forward to the contact, and always prepared lunch to celebrate the occasion.

In the interval since the previous visit with the nurse, Mrs. Apple, Mrs. Buck's neighbor, noticed a change in her friend. Out of concern, she made it a point to approach the nurse at the front of the building before she rang Mrs. Buck's buzzer. Mrs. Apple confided that Mrs. Buck was no longer getting out to shop and was definitely less energetic. Also, Mrs. Apple expressed concern about her friend's loss of weight, complaints about a change in her bowel habits, and her inability to sleep. She reported that Mrs. Buck had asked her niece to take her to her doctor, but this had not occurred.

Mrs. Apple also said that she had tried calling the niece several times, and had left urgent messages on her answering machine, but never got a return phone call. Also, Mrs. Apple claimed that Mrs. Buck had paid her niece not only to take care of financial matters but also to arrange for help in the home. Apparently these arrangements were never made. Mrs. Apple raised the possibility of theft, as she recalled that her friend once had significant savings but now seemed unable or unwilling to spend even the most modest amounts on herself. Mrs. Apple then requested that all of this information be kept confidential, claiming that "my friendship with her would change forever if she knew I said anything."

One look at Mrs. Buck confirmed Mrs. Apple's description of her health status. Over lunch, the nurse asked her if she had any help at home. Mrs. Buck hesitated, but then admitted she could use a little help with shopping and cleaning. "I don't get around like I used to," she said, adding that her niece was working on finding her help. When the nurse asked how long the niece had been working on this, tears welled up in her clients eyes. She said quietly, "I didn't want to bring it up but I can't hold it in anymore. She's my only relative, you see. My sister's little girl. I just don't know what to do."

Mrs. Buck proceeded to tell the nurse what Mrs. Apple had earlier disclosed, but did not mention a word about the possibility of her niece taking her money. When asked about this, Mrs. Buck exclaimed, "I can't believe Cynthia would ever do such a thing."

DELIA BUCK—A NURSE'S PERSPECTIVE

Terry Fulmer, Ph.D., R.N.
Associate Director,
Harvard Geriatric Education Center;
Associate Professor,
Boston College School of Nursing

The case of Mrs. Delia Buck illustrates many important concepts relative to the issues of exploitation and elder neglect. There are several aspects of this case that should be highlighted before one comes to a conclusion about whether exploitation or neglect have, in fact, occurred. The visiting nurse is in the fortunate position of having already established a trusting relationship with Mrs. Buck, and she is therefore in an ideal position to provide help and develop a long-term plan.

Of utmost importance is the fact that Mrs. Buck is a competent individual. There are no indicators that suggest that she has had any change in mental status or that she is exhibiting signs and symptoms of an acute confusional state. Since we only know the information presented in the case, it is important that this perception regarding Mrs. Buck's competence be validated by a professional before an elder abuse report is made. Competency is an issue in this case because it is important to confirm that Mrs. Buck's perception about the frequency with which her niece calls or visits is, in fact, correct; second, it is important to determine who would have power-of-attorney should she not be competent. Given the fact that Mrs. Buck is exhibiting signs and symptoms of deterioration in her health (such as the loss of energy, loss of weight, change in bowel habits, and change in sleeping patterns), it may be that there is a physiologic problem or disease state that is affecting her perceptual abilities. These same symptoms might also be related to depression, which could also be a factor in the way she perceives her current situation.

This is a difficult case because the abuse in question is exploitation that may be contributing to neglect. In and of itself, financial exploitation can be proven rather easily. As soon as the appropriate bank accounts are reviewed, it should be clear how funds are being used or misused. To prove that the misuse of funds then led to the neglect of an elderly person can be extremely difficult. With aging, it is common to have a number of chronic diseases as well as age-related changes that may exhibit themselves in ways that are similar to signs and symptoms of neglect. For example, the case discusses the fact that Mrs. Buck has had a change in her sleeping pattern. With normal aging, REM sleep decreases and wakeful periods throughout the night increase. This may be interpreted by the elderly individual as a "problem with sleep." It is also known that there is a pattern in older people in which their usual wake-up time in the morning occurs at earlier and earlier times. These are examples of normal age changes that may be interpreted as changes that result from neglect. It is noted that Mrs. Buck has had a decrease in energy. This may come from a decrease in her dietary intake secondary to the fact that she is unable to get out and do her shopping. Perhaps a case could be made that this weight loss is due to neglectful behavior on the part of her niece in that she has been less and less helpful in terms of assisting Mrs. Buck with her activities of daily living. At this point, however, there is not enough information to know.

The case states that Ms. Philips used to visit her aunt often and now she visits "less frequently." This is another area upon which it is difficult to make a judgment. Since Ms. Philips is not a guardian for Mrs. Buck, she has no legal obligation to visit her aunt more regularly, and as it has been pointed out, Mrs. Buck says "my niece has given so much of her time . . . she has her own life to live, you know." We would need more information about the usual life of Ms. Philips in order to understand better what her capabilities are. However, even if she had a large amount of time to spend with her aunt, the question still remains: What are her responsibilities? In the absence of a formal guardianship, she has no legal responsibilities to visit her aunt and really only has an ethical responsibility, which she may or may not feel. This is a difficult area to assess in the field of elder abuse and neglect. There are times when it seems that it would be appropriate for a certain family member to "pitch-in" and give care when an elderly person needs it; however, there are no rules in society about what family members should or should not do within the context of their own family dynamics. It seems that it would be very important for the visiting nurse to meet with Cynthia Philips in order to ascertain her perception about the situation and her own day-to-day responsibilities.

Mrs. Buck is also exhibiting signs and symptoms of recurrent cancer. With a change in bowel habits and decrease in energy, it may be that she is having a recurrence of her colon cancer and the visiting nurse has the responsibility to provide follow-up for that situation. It is also clear that Mrs. Buck is asking for help in relation to her shopping and cleaning. It seems that it would be fairly straightforward for the visiting nurse to arrange for a homemaker or home health aide to assist Mrs. Buck in her activities of daily living. This would also serve the important function of providing company for Mrs. Buck and, at the same time, provide a health care surveillance mechanism in order see that Mrs. Buck has her nutrition, rest, and comfort needs met.

The case mentions that Mrs. Buck once had significant savings but now seems unable or unwilling to spend even the most modest sums on herself. It is important to understand the difference between "unwilling" versus "unable." If Mrs. Buck is unable to spend the money, perhaps she is in financial difficulty and it would be important to understand where her money is being spent. If she is unwilling to spend this money, perhaps it is a pattern of lifetime spending behavior that is consistent with her behavior in younger life. In all cases in which there is a suspicion of abuse, neglect, or exploitation, it is important to discern the elderly person's lifelong patterns of behavior in order to determine whether or not they are consistent in late life. It may well be that Mrs. Buck had never been a person who has spent money on herself and she may feel that getting a person in to help her cook and clean is excessive or wasteful. It would be helpful to get more information from her about how she feels about spending money for services in the home.

Once the nurse had spoken to Mrs. Buck about her niece and the possibility of theft, Mrs. Buck makes the statement that she cannot believe Cynthia would ever do such a thing, referring to the fact that she does not believe Cynthia would ever steal her money. Obviously, the nurse's inquiry is upsetting to Mrs. Buck and she seems to have great faith in her niece. The nurse has a responsibility to check with Mrs. Buck in order to find out if it is okay with her to examine her financial matters with her niece. It may be that Mrs. Buck will refuse to let people check her financial matters, and this is her right as an autonomous adult.

Happily, the case has made no mention of nursing home placement as a possible alternative for Mrs. Buck's care. Frequently, when an elderly person is failing in the home setting, nursing home placement is one of the first options considered. This is unfortunate because it may be that the elderly person would rather suffer any amount of exploitation in order to avoid such placement. The visiting nurse needs to be extremely sensitive in this matter and assure Mrs. Buck that her wishes will be respected; if it is her wish to remain in the home setting with home care, every effort will be made to respect those wishes. It seems that an appropriate short-term care plan would be to hold a family conference with Mrs. Buck, Cynthia, and the visiting nurse in order to get a clear understanding of the situation. We have no information that would suggest that Cynthia has refused to meet with the visiting nurse. We know only that she is not returning Mrs. Apple's calls for whatever reason. In such a meeting, the three individuals could explore together what Mrs. Buck's needs are in order to understand what her actual home health care requirements might be. At that point, the nurse could ask Cynthia about financial arrangements and get a sense about the amount of money available to provide services for Mrs. Buck. Financial matters should be discussed in a long-term way, both because of the expense of home health aides and in order to help Mrs. Buck understand how long she could expect to afford such home care. Long-term care plans may involve liquidating some of Mrs. Buck's assets in order to pay for the services she requires.

It seems that a major difficulty in the case of Mrs. Buck is that of ineffective communication. The nurse has not yet spoken to Mrs. Buck's niece and she has not yet had the opportunity to explore with Mrs. Buck the etiology of the signs and symptoms that are being discussed. In most states, a visiting nurse has the responsibility to report any suspected cases of abuse, neglect, or exploitation. A dilemma that visiting nurses face is that in the event that they do make a report, it may cause a great deal of disruption in the life of the elderly person. For example, in this case, if the visiting nurse does make a report, it is likely that a protective service worker will go out and speak to Mrs. Buck, as well as try to speak to Mrs. Buck's niece and her neighbor, Mrs. Apple. This type of interrogation can be extremely stressful for all members involved, and an element of suspicion and distrust can then develop between the visiting nurse and the other parties. They may feel that they cannot speak freely to the visiting nurse without the fear of "a report," and it may be that there will be what is commonly known as a "conspiracy of silence" in order to keep the situation a private family matter instead of having it come to the attention of social service and protective service agencies. In any case that involves an elderly person, it is important to be sure that the plan is being made *with them*—not *for them*—so that their needs and wishes are being respected. In the event that the nurse feels that competency is an issue, then the process shifts to one that is more paternalistic.

This case is an excellent one for another reason. It illustrates the subtleness with which a case of exploitation or neglect may present itself. We have very little information to go on. We know only that there is a concerned neighbor who feels that her friend is deteriorating and also feels that perhaps there is a misuse of funds. The visiting nurse is presented with this information from this well-meaning neighbor and has yet to get information from the niece, and really needs to gather more information from Mrs. Buck as well. However, the important point to stress is that the common practice at this point in time is to overlook such subtleties. Health care professionals often assume that there is only smoke and no fire. Each year there is an increasing awareness of the fact that elder abuse, neglect, or exploitation may occur, and this has served to heighten the awareness on the part of health care professionals. Such awareness is changing the way situations are viewed; it is also changing the threshold of reporting. Some states have documented that there is now a trend toward overreporting of cases of elder abuse, neglect, or exploitation. It may be that there will be an era of overreporting before we come to understand some typical scenarios that warrant reports. It may also be that there will never be a typical scenario, and that the most prudent approach to a suspected case of elder abuse is simply to report in order to ensure that the elderly person gets the help of individuals who will be able to put this situation in a broader context. It may also be that this overreporting phenomenon will hurt the elderly. A report can cause hard feelings between care providers and the elders with whom they work, and they also serve to create barriers between elderly people and relatives who are remote, such as Mrs. Buck's niece. The limited responsibility that Cynthia Philips now feels for her aunt may decrease dramatically in the light of a protective service worker's interrogation. It seems that a careful approach is warranted in order to maintain whatever delicate balance is present. It seems that the hallmark of successful interventions in cases of elder mistreatment is consistent with the code of medical ethics set forth long ago by Hippocrates in that the norm should continue to be "do no harm."

DELIA BUCK—AN ATTORNEY'S PERSPECTIVE

Edmund F. Dejowski, J.D., Ph.D.
Institute for Health, Health Care Policy,
and Aging Research,
New Brunswick, New Jersey

Good legal advocacy, like good casework, proceeds step by step and in proper sequence. The exploitation issue is not yet timely in this case. Mrs. Buck has immediate unmet health care and daily living needs that are endangering her. These should be the focus of any intervention. An interrogation of Mrs. Buck on the issue of financial exploitation is likely to be met with an overcautious, deceptive, or hostile attitude. Furthermore, it is unnecessary; the client has already identified some of her most pressing needs, both to see a doctor and to get a little help shopping and cleaning. She is asking for urgently needed services that in themselves would considerably reduce her level of risk. The request for medical attention should be met first, while the client is fully cooperative. Next, finances should be probed naturally and easily in the context of the nurse's need to know particular pieces of information in order to arrange payment for home care.

Mrs. Buck's response to the discussion of finances is likely to shape the direction that the case will take. If exploitation is occurring, any one of several scenarios is likely.

If Mrs. Buck's money is gone, my guess is that she will want to conceal the fact, and will refuse home care once she understands that in order to qualify for public funded services she will have to show what became of her money. She may say she can afford to pay, but has decided she no longer wants the service.

On the other hand, Mrs. Buck may acknowledge that the money is gone, but refuse to say where it went; or she may be vague and inconsistent about what happened to it; or she may confide the whole story, the following one being one of the toughest case scenarios for the service provider: "I signed over my bank account to my niece. She promised to use it get me services, but she's spending it on her boyfriend instead. I don't care what happens to me any more. I won't do anything to cause my niece trouble. She's welcome to keep the money if she wants it that bad."

If evidence accumulates that Mrs. Buck is the victim of financial exploitation (or even if she has just mismanaged her own affairs), can the nurse arrange to have someone else manage Mrs. Buck's finances for her?

"Substituted judgment" is the process whereby one individual is empowered with authority to make legally binding decisions on behalf of another. Some mechanisms for substituted judgment are available only if Mrs. Buck suffers from impaired judgment. Such devices as guardianship, conservatorship, or protective orders require documentation of such impairments in court. The record here does not suggest that Mrs. Buck is judgmentally impaired. The nurse should become well acquainted with the legal definition of mental impairment so that she or he can recognize it, using objective criteria in addition to clinical skills.

But even if Mrs. Buck were mentally incapacitated, the state law may not authorize the nurse to petition for the appointment of a guardian. Most likely, the nurse would need to involve the Adult Protective Services agency in Mrs. Buck's locality if a guardianship was thought appropriate, and if it was felt the niece could not be trusted, since there are no other relatives to serve as petitioners.

A growing number of states are implementing laws that make it easier for a temporary guardian to be appointed during the period that the petition is pending. This is important because the niece could dispose of all of Mrs. Buck's assets before the court ever decides whether to appoint a guardian.

If the court does appoint a guardian or conservator, he or she will have full access to Mrs. Buck's financial records, and will be able to make decisions in her interest, even if she disagrees with them.

If Mrs. Buck is competent, but is willing to permit the nurse or another party to handle her finances, she can grant a power-of-attorney or establish a joint bank account. Both of these devices require that she be competent at the time she signs them. The power-of-attorney, furthermore, becomes invalid the moment Mrs. Buck becomes incapacitated, which severely limits its usefulness. A few states permit the power to be made "durable," that is, to remain effective even after the onset of incapacity. In some states it can be made "springing," that is, it will become effective only when and if Mrs. Buck becomes mentally or physically incapacitated.

We don't know whether Mrs. Buck receives social security, but she probably does. The nurse should inquire. If it unfolds that Mrs. Buck has been mismanaging her social security payments (for example, by giving them to her niece), the nurse can request that the Social Security Administration name a "representative payee" to receive and manage Mrs. Buck's monthly checks. This does not require that Mrs. Buck be incompetent, just that she show a history of mismanagement and a disability affecting her capacity to manage the funds properly on her own behalf. No court proceedings are involved, and it may be done against the wishes of Mrs. Buck (although, of course, she has a right to contest and present her side). Similar arrangements are possible for SSI, railroad retirement benefits, Veterans Administration benefits, Black Lung Disease benefits and Department of Defense pensions.

If Mrs. Buck is competent but uncooperative, are there any legal remedies against someone who might be exploiting her? A brief overview of the legal issues in financial exploitation may help clarify the range of options.

Under traditional legal concepts, cheating someone out of their money, stealing it, or using it for yourself without their permission is each a violation of both criminal and civil law.

In civil law—in which one individual can sue another to recover something, or ask a court to order or prohibit something—the injured party must bring the action. Where a competent victim is unwilling to bring and pursue a suit, there can be no remedy.

The state, however, has the right to bring charges against a person suspected of violations of criminal law, even if the victim refuses to cooperate. But it is unlikely that this will happen. For one thing, if the victim proved a weak and unwilling witness, the evidence would have to be very strong to gain a conviction. For another, prosecutors are likely to give a great deal of deference to the victim's wishes in deciding whether to prosecute.

If Mrs. Buck does not cooperate, neither the traditional civil nor criminal remedies would appear viable, even if we could establish wrongdoing by the niece. However, if Mrs. Buck is adjudicated to be impaired judgmentally and a guardian is appointed, the guardian may have the authority to bring a civil action against the niece to seek damages or to prohibit future exploitation.

Some states have been experimenting with new laws that more directly address such issues as financial exploitation. Some have made it a crime, for example, to exploit an older or disabled person. Such laws may make it easier to prosecute exploiters of persons who will not or cannot bring charges. In some states, third parties, such as public officials, may petition for court orders to prevent or stop exploitation.

Such an order, for example, might require the niece to cease spending Mrs. Buck's money. Because the proceeding is civil, and not criminal, a lower level of proof is required, making the relief much easier to attain than a criminal conviction would be. The nurse should know about the particular remedies for exploitation that are available in her or his state, and as the case and the evidence develop further, may need to consider such a remedy.

A pertinent but controversial question involves the circumstances under which the law may impose a legal obligation to provide care to another. For example, must grown children provide care for disabled parents? Is a niece committing a crime if she walks out and abandons an aunt who has been relying on her for essential care? Laws to impose such obligation generally have not proven effective or enforceable, and this area of law is not yet well developed.

Simple commonsense plans and practical compromises may be less poignant than legal solutions but are usually the best remedies available. The nurse should never allow the injustice and intrigue of possible financial exploitation or neglect to deflect her attention from meeting Mrs. Buck's immediate service needs.

If there is no indication of incapacity, Mrs. Buck has every right to make foolish choices for herself; but this need not stop the nurse from offering counseling on how and why Mrs. Buck should protect her own interests.

DELIA BUCK—STUDY QUESTIONS

(1) Detection
    (a)   What are the indicators of financial exploitation? Neglect?
    (b)   What questions should the worker ask to gather more information about the possibility of financial exploitation? Neglect?
    (c)   What is the best way to structure the interview in order to elicit information about possible exploitation and neglect?

(2) Assessment
    (a)   What is the evidence that financial exploitation and/or neglect has occurred?
    (b)   Is there any indication that there is a pattern of exploitation or neglect?
    (c)   What questions should be asked to ascertain frequency, severity, and a history of exploitation and neglect? How do the answers to these questions influence case planning?
    (d)   What is the cause of the exploitation and neglect? If the etiologies

are unclear, what questions should the nurse ask to gain a better understanding? Why is this knowledge important?

(e) How long has the exploitation and neglect been going on (if, of course, it exists at all)? If this is unclear, what questions should be asked to ascertain this information?

(f) What are possible explanations for why Mrs. Buck is talking about her problems now?

(g) How much information is needed about the niece in order to help Mrs. Buck?

(h) How much information is needed about Mrs. Buck's support network in order to help her?

(i) What is the etiology of Mrs. Buck's loss of function (e.g., recurrence of colon cancer, depression due to loss of sleep)? How should the nurse further assess these problems?

(3) Interventions

(a) What are possible short-term case plans?

(b) What are possible long-term case plans?

(c) Who should the nurse consult with in order to make these case plans?

(d) How would Mrs. Buck's perception of her problems influence case planning?

(e) What are the hallmarks of successful interventions?

(f) Are there intervention pitfalls the nurse should be aware of?

(g) What are the legal determinants of neglect? Can it be prosecuted? Do the laws differ from state to state?

(h) Is moving for guardianship for Mrs. Buck appropriate? Why or why not?

(i) How do state laws impact on investigating financial exploitation and neglect and intervening in such cases?

JULIA STONE—CASE STUDY

Jane Cunningham, a social worker with a small, local senior center, was working on the next month's activity schedule when two center members knocked on her door. She knew both of them fairly well, as they had been members for over a year and attended regularly. She welcomed them into her office, and when they both stood near her desk looking at each other anxiously, she offered them chairs, closed the door, and sat down near them. "What's up?" Jane asked.

Mary, a healthy, active woman in her early seventies, recently widowed, did the talking. "I told Julia that she must talk with you because it's nonsense what she's been going through and it's been going on too long!" Julia Stone, a woman in her late sixties, was short of breath and had a history of emphysema. As she played with a loose thread on her sleeve, she looked down and spoke: "I'm okay, really. It's just this condition. I just don't have the energy or patience I used to have." Mary interrupted: "Your son is a louse—making you walk to the center in the rain today."

Julia, visibly upset and almost in tears, said in a quivering voice, "He needed my car to go on a job interview today. He needs to get a job." Jane, leaning toward Julia, said, "I wish you had called me. I could have arranged transportation for you. You know this; I've done it for you before."

Julia nodded her head slowly, saying, "He's a good boy, you know." Again, Mary jumped in: "Look at you! You're out of breath, a nervous wreck, exhausted because he keeps you up all night, and you call him a 'good boy'!"

"When he doesn't take his medications he gets this way," said Julia. "So wild. He doesn't mean to be mean to me. I'm his mother." Looking at Jane, she added, "He just needs a new psychiatrist. One who will help him this time."

Jane looked at Julia and said, "I didn't know life was so difficult for you at home," and added that she was glad Julia had come in to tell her. Mary blurted, "I had to force her to come in here. Look at her! Her shoes are soaking wet!"

Jane looked down at Julia's feet and asked if she was uncomfortable or cold. Julia said she wasn't and didn't want to be any trouble. Jane brought the space heater closer to Julia's feet.

"How does he keep you up, Julia?," Jane asked.

"Well, you know, when he's on his medications he's fine, a fine boy. But off of them he's different. He sleeps all day, and then he's up all night. He comes into my room after midnight and wants to know where things are. He turns on my light and says, 'Ma, where are the scissors?' or 'Ma, don't you buy bread for the house anymore?' Then, I'm awake, answering questions and hearing him clamor around the house. When I ask him to leave me alone, he starts using foul language and says nasty things and that scares me. And that music he plays is so loud. My neighbors complain but he doesn't turn it down."

Julia stopped talking; there was a short silence as she looked out the window. She looked back at Jane with tears in her eyes and said, "I love my son; he was so good to me when my husband died. He needs a new psychiatrist. You know of one, don't you?"

JULIA STONE—A SOCIAL WORKER'S PERSPECTIVE

Brenda Stiefel, CSW
Former Project Director of the
Victim Services Agency's Elder Abuse Project
New York City

Elder mistreatment occurs within the framework of the family. The victims in these situations are often burdened by a sense of guilt. Julia Stone is unsure as to how to relate to her abusive son and is continually anxious about his behavior. She is clearly confused by her son's behavior and is in conflict with her maternal instincts to protect him.

Consequently, initial conversations with Julia about possible abuse must be undertaken with the greatest sensitivity. It is important for the social worker to determine whether privacy is essential for Julia before she can begin to tell her story. Would Mary's presence help her or be an intrusion? The social worker may prefer to see Julia privately to assure her that the case would be handled confidentially. Since Julia has been a member of the center for awhile, she may think that receiving counseling there will stigmatize her. The social worker might even suggest a location away from the center for their initial meeting. Or, another approach, if it is acceptable to Julia, would be to invite Mary to participate in the discussion.

It is important to take a nonjudgmental approach when counseling victims. For example, Julia expressed deep concern for her son. Should the worker criticize her son sharply, Julia may become alienated. Nevertheless, routine questions must be asked and the client's answers need to be examined closely. How long has the client been living under the present circumstances (whether alone or with a particular family member)? What factors brought about the mistreatment (i.e., relocation, divorce, health problems, death)?

The worker should attempt to determine the cause of Julia's abuse and when it started. Julia had previously indicated that problems and confusion in the family arose at the time of her husband's death. What tensions did this event cause within the family? When Julia's husband died, she may have lost significant emotional and economic support and physical protection. This loss may be expressed in prolonged grief or depression, especially if there were no other relationships to substitute for this loss.

Does the client have any other children, family members, or other support? Does she find the family supportive or difficult to talk to? Nonabusing family members may also be under a considerable stress related to the mistreatment and may be in need of assistance. The original case study revealed that Julia's neighbors had started to complain about the son's abusive language and his loud music. It may be possible to work with the neighbors and change the nature of their involvement to that of helping the victim.

As part of the initial interview, the social worker could discuss statistics related to elder mistreatment as a way of making clear to Julia that her situation is not so unusual. If isolation is a problem for Julia, the worker could attempt to increase her contact with others and to provide opportunities for socialization.

Victims often come forward for the sake of the abuser rather than themselves. The ability to respond to a request for help for the abuser may be precluded by the limitations of a particular agency. In such cases, the social worker could recommend an appropriate agency and coordinate with other professionals, although frequently abusers refuse assistance. Julia may feel totally responsible for her son and therefore would not consider an Order of Protection. If, however, immediate relocation is necessary for Julia, a shelter may be a temporary solution. It may not be the ideal alternative, but may be the only safe option available. Julia may be disappointed or angry because the options offered to her may not be satisfactory or services she would prefer may not be available. Indeed, in many localities there are significant gaps in service that limit the options for victims of elder mistreatment.

In Julia's case, her friend Mary literally brings her to the social worker and begins telling the story of abuse for her. Often it may be difficult to ascertain the facts related to an abusive situation. Usually, careful questioning must be carried out to reveal the true circumstances surrounding the potential abuse. "Is your child doing things that you can no longer tolerate? Have you had any injuries that have required medical attention?" This kind of direct questioning will help the client realize that the worker is able and willing to discuss such sensitive issues with her.

Finally, the social worker may want to make a home visit. Caution should be taken during any home visits with elder abuse victims, since their homes are frequently unsafe. Even in cases of suspected abuse or when clients have specifically denied its occurrence, caution must always be employed. For safety reasons, it may be necessary for the social worker to make the home visit with another worker or the police, or to devise some other safety strategy before proceeding to the home alone.

Short-term planning, long-term counseling, and specific, ongoing supportive services may help to raise a client's self-esteem and strengthen his or her mechanisms of coping. The social worker's primary responsibility is to the person who has been mistreated. By listening closely to the elder abuse victim, and by offering specific and available remedies and options, the social worker conveys a sincere message of encouragement and support. A trusting relationship is the foundation from which all future work will be based. But, hopefully, the helping process will move the client toward positive change, which can be frightening initially, but ultimately beneficial.

JULIA STONE—AN ATTORNEY'S PERSPECTIVE

Kerry Baron, J.D.
Chief, Landlord/Tenant Crime Unit;
formally Supervisor, Sex Crimes/Special Victims Bureau,
District Attorney, Kings County, New York

(The following are the opinions of Mr. Baron, and not necessarily those of the Brooklyn District Attorney's office.)

Can the social or health service professional aid Julia Stone by resorting to the legal system? Before we can answer this question, we must understand what the system is and how it functions.

Unlike social and health service principles, which can be applied universally, there is a multitude of legal systems, and systems within systems. The laws of one state do not necessarily correspond to the laws of any other state.

In this example, if Julia Stone were in New York State, she might seek to have her son prosecuted for a violation of the law known as "harassment." In New York, this can be found in the criminal code called the Penal Law at section 240.25. This offense may be prosecuted in the local criminal court, but it is not a crime. In California, no similar criminal law exists. Annoying and alarming conduct is defined and prohibited in California's Code of Civil Procedure at section 527.6. In California, however, there is a specific section, Penal Law section 368, which codifies an entire category of actions that, when committed against "elders," constitutes a crime. New York has no similar statute. One can readily see that advice to Julia Stone must be tailored according to where she lives. Also, if she is visiting outside her normal jurisdiction, then the advice given her should reflect the legal system of the new jurisdiction. Such advice, tailored to the laws of a different state, might be different than the advice normally given.

Occasionally, this "system" is further complicated by the existence of different prosecution offices servicing the same area. In Los Angeles, the county prosecuting attorney (district attorney) prosecutes felonies, while the city attorney prosecutes misdemeanors. Add to this the complication that prosecutors have "prosecutorial discretion," the ability to prosecute or refuse to prosecute cases. The district attorney "downstate" may prosecute something an "upstate" district attorney would ignore. How can you cope with this?

Don't panic. This sounds more complicated than it really is. An approach to this problem is to get together with a group of professionals sharing similar interests and invite an attorney or prosecutor to talk to you about your local legal system. Many will gladly do this free of charge. For a government official, it is good public relations; for a local attorney, it is free "advertising."

Do not let the talk, however, degenerate into a mere civics lesson. You want specific information, such as what type of case will be prosecuted. Ask for the names, section numbers, and descriptions of those laws (or crimes) defining conduct relating to threats and annoying or alarming behavior. Ask about conduct in which there is a minor slap, push, or shove, or in which injury is minimal. Then, after you understand the laws that govern most of your factual situations, ask about other crimes—serious assaults, robberies, larcenies, and sexual offenses.

The reason for proceeding this way is simple. Lawyers work with words in a precise fashion. If the words of your client do not establish the specific elements of the crime, the case cannot proceed. In New York, for example, the threat "I'll kill you" may at best be the violation of the previously mentioned harassment law. The New York police cannot make an arrest for such an offense unless it was committed in their presence. However, if you asked your client whether her son had brandished any object in his hand while he threatened her, then he may have committed the crime of menacing (a misdemeanor), for which the police in New York can arrest him upon your client's recitation of the facts. If you had been unaware of the elements of the crime, her mere statement describing a threat, while seeming sufficiently significant to you, would not have the same significance to an attorney.

Let us apply this technique while reexamining the fact pattern regarding Julia Stone and the unavailable car. We know that her son has the car. We know he needed it; she stated that. Yet she said nothing of how he got the car. Is there a crime? The first question might be, how did her son obtain the keys? Did he take them out of her pocketbook or off of her dresser without her permission? Is expressed permission the required custom in her house? Did he grab the keys out of her hand? Was she threatened? Was she hurt? The answers to these questions can suggest that his conduct ranged from inconsiderate, on the one hand, to assault and robbery, on the other.

The question still remains: Why bother with the legal system? If you can gain entry into your local legal system, you'll find that the courts have the ability to help your client significantly. The greatest help comes through the power of "coercion."

What does Julia Stone want? If she is similar to the vast majority of parents I have interviewed, she *doesn't want* her son to go to jail. She simply wants her son not to make loud noises, not to wake her up at night, not to harass her, and not to scare her. She also wants her son to take his psychiatric medicine. These are things she has repeatedly asked her son to do. And they are things that the court, with its coercive power, can direct her son to do.

Understand that the courts are not a panacea. But many persons, out of fear of court-imposed sanctions (being placed on probation, being directed to engage in free public work projects for a specified number of days, or ultimately, being sent to jail), will follow the simple rules of human behavior they otherwise ignore.

Most frequently the court directs this behavior by an Order of Protection or temporary restraining order. Depending upon the local legal system, these orders can direct a defendant to do almost anything, even require him or her to live somewhere else. Violation of the order will result in further legal difficulties for that person. For example, in California, the harassment section of the civil code permits the court to grant a restraining order, directing the defendant's conduct. Violation of the order permits prosecution for contempt of court in the criminal system. In New York, similarly, the family court's Order of Protection, when violated, can give rise to criminal prosecution.

In some respects, criminal prosecution affords more viable assistance to the victim. (Of course, as a prosecutor, my view may be slanted.) Cases are presented by the government's attorney free of any charge to the victim. The defendant is entitled to free legal defense, if needed. The criminal system, which once saw jail as its main remedy, now has a variety of diversionary programs available (such as counseling and psychiatric care). In some communities, even the criminal defense bar has social service programs to assist its clients. Some even find new places for their clients to live.

The key drawback to proceeding in the criminal system is the stigma of the criminal conviction. Many parents who initially needed the defendant arrested and out of the house will seek to drop the case because they do not want to see their child with a criminal record. To some extent, this withdrawal of prosecution by the victim has conditioned prosecutors (and police) and has caused them to shy away from prosecuting elder abuse (or domestic violence). Recently, the trend has reversed. Prosecutors' offices throughout the nation have specially trained assistants to help victims of domestic violence proceed in the courts. Some offices have even established special elder abuse/domestic violence units.

Proceeding in the criminal justice system does not necessitate a criminal record. In some jurisdictions, there exists a series of convictions that do not constitute crimes and are sealed from the public's eye. In others, there exists a system of lengthy adjournments conditioned upon specified behavior, which, when performed faithfully, will result in an outright dismissal of the case. These procedures may not have been designed for the domestic violence defendant, but they are frequently used in the prosecution of their cases.

There are, of course, noncriminal systems designed to handle elder mistreatment (and domestic violence) from a mental health or social service perspective. A further explanation of these systems, as well as of other noncriminal conviction alternatives, are among the questions to ask the attorney.

Regardless of the system chosen, one can be assured that with the more enlightened approach many communities are taking in the area of domestic violence, your client will be dealt with in a dignified fashion. You can enhance this by striving to remove from your client any stereotypical view she or he may have about the "law" and any guilt she or he may have about proceeding against relatives through the legal system.

JULIA STONE—STUDY QUESTIONS

(1) Detection

   (a) What are the indicators of abuse?

    (b) What questions should the worker ask to gather more information about the abuse situation?

    (c) What is the best way to structure the interview in order to elicit information about abuse? (For example, should Jane speak with Julia privately? What are the possible positive or negative repercussions of not asking Mary to leave?)

(2) Assessment

    (a) What is the evidence that abuse or neglect has occurred?

    (b) Is there any indication that there is a pattern of abuse?

    (c) What questions should be asked to ascertain frequency, severity, and history of abuse? How do the answers to these questions influence case planning?

    (d) What is the cause of abuse in this case? If etiology is unclear, what questions should the social worker ask to gain a better understanding of it? Why is this knowledge important?

    (e) How long has the abuse been going on? If this is unclear, what questions should be asked to ascertain this information? Is there any reason to suspect that stress on the family precipitated the onset of the abuse?

    (f) What are possible explanations for why Julia is talking about the abuse now?

    (g) How much information is needed about Julia's son in order to help Julia?

    (h) How much information is needed about other members of Julia's family and other support networks in order to help her?

(3) Interventions

    (a) What are possible short-term case plans?

    (b) What are possible long-term case plans?

    (c) How does Julia perceive the problem and how does this influence case planning?

    (d) What value systems might Julia be operating on which may color her perception of possible options? (For example, are there hints as to Julia's views on parenting that might contribute to feelings of shame, guilt, or self-blame? And if she has these feelings, would she use the courts? Why or why not?)

    (e) What are the hallmarks of successful interventions?

    (f) Are there any intervention pitfalls that workers should be aware of? (For example, knowing that the parent-child bond is often a strong one, the worker should avoid sounding judgmental of Julia's son, as this may alienate Julia.)

    (g) What are the possible legal options for Julia? (For example, obtaining an Order of Protection in family or criminal court.)

    (h) Would acting on any of these options have adverse consequences for either Julia or her son?

(i)   Why would an elder abuse victim use the courts? How is this helpful? What are the problems victims might confront in court and in using Orders of Protection?

(j)   When is an Order of Protection considered an appropriate legal option?

(k)   What are the court's expectations of those seeking protection?

(l)   What is the police role in enforcing Orders of Protection?

(m) What is the worker's role as advocate when helping a victim seek an Order of Protection?

(n)   What else can the court provide besides Orders of Protection?

(o)   What might a victim expect from an assistant district attorney?

(p)   Is a victim entitled to legal counsel in family court?

(q)   What aspects of these legal options vary from state to state? How does a worker become informed of his or her state laws?

(r)   How would a mandatory reporting law hurt or help Julia?

HOWARD WASHINGTON—CASE STUDY

Howard Washington, age 74, was hospitalized for an infected leg ulcer. He had a history of poor circulation in his lower extremities and had undergone two arterial bypass surgeries for this condition over the past seven years. Three years ago he was hospitalized for a heart attack and he still has chest pain that responds to medical therapy. For the last six months, he has been on multiple pain medications for the chronic leg pain and his greatest fear has been the possibility of amputation.

Even though the infection seemed to be improving after a full course of intravenous antibiotics, Mr. Washington claimed the pain was intolerable, and he had a diminished appetite and sleep disturbance. Before calling in a psychiatric consult for depressive features and concern about Mr. Washington's mental status, the physician telephoned Mrs. Washington to get a better understanding of Mr. Washington's home life. From the beginning of the conversation, Mrs. Washington stated frankly that she didn't want to talk about her husband and that she didn't want him to come home. But she did say that her husband suffered periods of mental confusion.

She went on to say that she had thought about divorcing her husband for most of their married life, that she had suffered a lot during the 40 years of their marriage and had put up with him only for the sake of their daughter, Liz. Mrs. Washington said that now that Liz was married, she thought it was time for her to get her own life in order and that her husband could fend for himself. "I'm 70 years old and I'm not getting any younger. After five years of getting him through two surgeries and nursing him at home and catering to his every wish and whim, I've got to start paying attention to my own health and peace of mind." Mrs. Washington claimed that her husband could live with their daughter, Liz.

After speaking with Mrs. Washington, the physician decided to speak with her patient directly. She told Mr. Washington of the conversation with his wife and asked him if he would rather live with his wife or daughter. Mr. Washington exclaimed, "My daughter's still at home— what do you mean?" After further discussion, Mr. Washington did recall that his daughter had recently married and moved out of the house. He seemed quite embarrassed to have forgotten that his daughter was married. The doctor then said that she wanted Mr. Washington to see a psychiatrist because of the problems with his memory and his obvious distress. Mr. Washington flatly refused.

The physician consulted with the social worker and asked him to find out if it would be possible for Mr. Washington to live with his daughter. The social worker telephoned Liz, who spoke at length about the impossibility of her father living with her; she had recently married and was not willing to disrupt her life for her father at this time. The nurses on the floor were not surprised by this response; they informed the social worker that although Liz visited her father several times a week, the conversations between them were almost always brief and strained.

Finding the daughter unreceptive to the idea of her father moving in, the social worker called Mrs. Washington with the hope of better understanding the conflict. Mrs. Washington informed him that she no longer wanted to talk about her husband, and if the hospital had any further questions, they could speak with her attorney.

The social worker told Mr. Washington of the developments. He firmly stated that he intended to be discharged home and that his wife could move out if she didn't like it. Approaching hysteria, Mr. Washington screamed, "Doesn't she know I could lose my leg? Doesn't she care? Doesn't she know what I'm going through?" He stated that he was sick and tired of the way his wife had been treating him, claiming, "She slapped me around before but now that I'm better, she's going to find out who's boss." He added that the hospital could speak with his lawyer if they didn't send him home.

The social worker met with his supervisor, at which time they decided to call a team meeting with the physician in charge, the head nurse, and the social worker to discuss the case and decide what to do next.

HOWARD WASHINGTON—A
SOCIAL WORKER'S PERSPECTIVE

Andrea Nevins, M.S.W.
Project Director,
Victim Services Agency/
Mt. Sinai Medical Center's
Elder Abuse Project,
New York City

(At the time this was written, Ms. Nevins was a geriatric social worker at Montefiore Medical Center, Bronx, New York.)

The case of Mr. Washington presents the social worker with many difficult questions. Significant medical and psychosocial issues are entangled in a web of long-standing, unresolved family conflicts. Mr. Washington and his family are clearly in crisis, and the hospital social worker must be clinically astute and develop clear goals and objectives for intervention to be effective.

Together with an interdisciplinary team, the social worker will need to assess Mr. Washington's physical and functional status, psychological state, emotional needs, support system, and economic resources. Risk factors should be identified and allegations of mistreatment explored. Ultimately, a determination will need to be made about whether abuse exists, and who the victim is. Early intervention will be essential in order to develop an appropriate discharge plan.

The social worker has two choices in approaching this case. (1) She can view Mr. Washington as her client and work toward a plan that accommodates his needs and safety. (2) She can view the family as a single primary treatment unit by addressing each individual's needs and safety concerns, and move toward an optimal outcome for all. This would probably require the kind of long-term intensive work that the hospital social worker is rarely in a position to undertake. If the former option is chosen, the social worker can begin the process in the hospital and refer the case to an appropriate community agency to continue the long-term work after discharge. Despite hospital pressures, the discharge should be delayed until a safe and appropriate plan is developed.

Since it is not clear in this case whether abuse and/or neglect is occurring, or, if so, who is the victim and who is the abuser, the social worker's assessment will be the key to guiding intervention.

Mr. Washington and his family members should be interviewed separately to allow for confidentiality and uninterfered communication. Neutrality should be relayed and the sharing of previously obtained information should be avoided. Similar inquiries should be made of each family member and any inconsistencies noted. We already suspect long-standing conflicts between family members; but the social worker might begin by inquiring why the family is in crisis *now*.

Fundamentally, the Washingtons are expressing anger and resentful feelings about "suffering" and being "stuck with each other" over the years. These expressions of frustrated aggression, coupled with the observed strained dynamics between father and daughter, are important signals that deserve serious attention. The possibility of abuse or neglect must be considered.

Ascertaining the cause of mistreatment will guide interventions. The following points should be considered in the social worker's assessment of Mr. Washington:

(1) Assessment of Mr. Washington's mental status. Perhaps his refusal of the recommended psychiatric evaluation is related to denial, anger, or embarrassment. Counseling around these feelings, and moving Mr. Washington toward an acceptance of such an evaluation, is a crucial task for the social worker, since Mr. Washington's questionable mental status may affect his decision-making abilities and hurt the outcome of the discharge planning process. A thorough assessment will determine the events that precipitated Mr. Washington's depression. He may be suffering from a pseudodementia, whereby his depression manifests in periods of confusion. However, despite what his family and consulting professionals might deem to be in his best interest, unless adjudicated "incompetent," Mr. Washington will be presumed able independently to make fundamental decisions as to where to live, with whom to live, how to spend time, and so on (Zuckerman & Dubler, 1986, pp. 4-5).

(2) Establishment of possible causal factors for abuse or neglect should be assessed by exploring Mrs. Washington's caretaking responsibilities. For example, if Mr. Washington is dependent on his wife for assistance, how does she fulfill this caretaking role? What is his understanding of the extent of his needs and what does he do when those needs are not sufficiently met? What are his expectations and are they realistic? What are hers? This information will be helpful in assessing whether Mrs. Washington is even informed about available support services and if aware, whether she is deliberately creating an isolated environment for which mistreatment could continue unnoticed. Determination of financial resources and how they are managed will also help in identifying whether defined needs are being met and if they are being properly allocated.

Given the initial case summary, one might wonder whether Liz is a resentful daughter who may have been abused as a child or witnessed scenes of domestic violence. Perhaps the angry wife, Mrs. Washington, was herself the victim of spousal mistreatment. Clearly, she is exhausted and frustrated by the responsibilities of her caretaking role. Mrs. Washington may also have feelings of depression connected with unresolved conflicts or perhaps guilt about a failing marriage and the breaking up of the family unit, creating the necessity for new living arrangements at this stage of her life.

As with Mr. Washington, the social worker's psychosocial assessment of Mrs. Washington should explore roles, relationships with her husband and daughter, financial resources, and personal activities (to identify sources of outside relief). In assessing allegations of mistreatment (by either party), the following points should be explored:

- If Mrs. Washington is the primary caretaker, determine her responsibilities and her capability of fulfilling them.
- Inquire as to expectations, difficulties, and frustrations of her caretaking role. For example, how does or doesn't she cope? Has she ever mistreated Mr. Washington in any way?
- Evaluate her satisfaction and the quality of relationships with her husband and daughter. Probe further about the "suffering" she describes. For example, was she abused? Did she ever tell anyone or take formal action? Why has she stayed in the relationship (e.g., guilt, economic dependence, fear of emotional damage to daughter, lack of alternatives, fear of retaliation)?
- Inquire as to potential causal factors for marital and familial conflicts (e.g., alcoholism/drug abuse, psychopathology, transgenerational violence).
- Finally, question why she is insistent on taking action now (i.e., did something precipitate this crisis)?

If possible, Liz Washington should also be interviewed. Perhaps she could clarify inconsistencies as to her parent's behavior and lifestyle and lend additional information to the social worker's assessment. She might describe the family dynamics and her ability or inability to mediate between her parents.

As a result of time pressures, the social worker's initial assessment will form the basis for any short- or long-term planning. Intervention and discharge planning will rely heavily upon Mr. Washington's mental and functional status, which are unclear at this point.

When intervening with cases of elder mistreatment and neglect, the following principles are suggested as general guidelines: (1) respect for the client's self-determination if mentally competent, (2) maintenance of the family unit, whenever possible, (3) use of the "least restrictive alternative" in planning by using community-based services rather than institutionalization, whenever possible, and (4) avoidance of blame. Inadequate or inappropriate intervention might be worse than none at all.

With the tremendous resistance toward remaining together, it is possible that the most anxiety-provoking issues raised by the Washingtons for the social worker are their statements about resorting to legal action rather than working together toward a less extreme resolution. Although there is a tendency to think that children are responsible for care of their parents, there is actually no law of filial responsibility.

The social worker should encourage the seeking of legal advice to discuss eviction rights and the process of separation. Pursuit of a separation (with or without divorce proceedings) would probably need to be settled in court. If Mr. Washington is adjudicated "incompetent," or if his mental status remains questionable, his allegations might not be taken seriously in court without an advocate.

Proceedings for permanent separation and housing alternatives should only be a last resort, when no other options exist and the living situation remains dangerous to either Mr. or Mrs. Washington. If a temporary situation is necessary, given the high tension levels, the optimal plan would be for one or the other to stay with their daughter (if she changes her mind and agrees to this) or with other relatives or friends, or in a residential facility. This might provide a "cooling-off" period to allow more time for planning. Given time constraints, this "interim" plan might be the most practical approach, with the hope that concrete assistance and ongoing counseling will help the couple move toward resolution of certain conflicts and healthy alternative behaviors.

Given Mr. Washington's potential for further medical complications and his increased vulnerability, the social worker and interdisciplinary team will need to explore with the Washingtons the options available for care, and the possibility of utilizing resources to meet defined needs.

Given the multitude of problems and the fact of time constraints, short-term goals should address the immediate problems. They might include:

- provision for emotional support for Mr. Washington regarding his family conflicts, severe pain, and fear of further medical complications
- education for the family about the etiology and effects of elder mistreatment and the development of coping and behavior alternatives

- possible assistance by Liz Washington in fulfilling a mediating role between her parents
- supportive counseling and assistance for Mrs. Washington in clarifying and meeting personal needs
- education of the couple about options and available resources and counseling toward the acceptance of outside assistance (e.g., home health care service, adult day care, Meals-on-Wheels, respite care) to help maximize quality of care for Mr. Washington and to minimize his wife's stress and responsibilities as a caretaker
- exploration of financial assistance if eligible (e.g., senior citizen or income-eligible entitlements), or financial management to prevent exploitation (e.g., power-of-attorney)
- exploration of legal intervention if necessary (e.g., obtaining an Order of Protection, or appointment of a conservator, as appropriate, to ensure proper allocation of resources and provision of needed services)
- referral to a protective service or other social services agency to assist in case management and monitoring of the potential risk situation

Undoubtedly, work with this case will be a challenging, perhaps frustrating, and complex process. Engaging the family should lead to a thorough assessment of causal factors for the alleged mistreatment, and the results of this evaluation should lend way to appropriate intervention options.

HOWARD WASHINGTON—A
PHYSICIAN'S PERSPECTIVE

Pat A. Bloom, M.D.
Director of Curriculum Development in Geriatrics
Albert Einstein College of Medicine
and Montefiore Medical Center

In this case, as in any case of suspected elder mistreatment, a complex array of symptoms and signs raises the suspicion of abuse. It is the responsibility of the physician or other health professional who first comes in contact with the patient to think about the possibility of abuse or neglect, and to initiate a comprehensive investigation, usually by a team of health care professionals, to confirm or disprove this suspicion. In this case, there is a clear indication of abuse in the statements made by both Mr. and Mrs. Washington: His statement that he has been "slapped around" and hers that she has "suffered a lot" because of her marriage. Without further investigation, it is impossible to ascertain which person, if either, is a victim of abuse, but it is important to entertain the possibility that either or both could be.

Physicians, nurses, and other health care professionals need to learn more about the problem of elder abuse and neglect, especially when to suspect it. At our medical center, we have focused our initial educational efforts on the emergency room staff. Victims of abuse frequently report to emergency rooms for treatment of their injuries, whether they are admitted to the hospital or not; furthermore, victims who are reluctant to recognize or confront their situations "hop" from one emergency room to another in order to maintain anonymity and prevent recognition of a pattern of injuries. Points of the history and physical examination that our emergency room staff have been trained to consider in raising the possibility of abuse or neglect include:

Client History and Background

(1) patient reports abuse or neglect
(2) conflicting stories
(3) long interval between injury and seeking care
(4) physician "hopping"
(5) patient dependent for care
(6) patient depended upon for medical care, financial support, or emotional support by family member
(7) history of similar episodes
(8) history of mental illness, family violence, substance abuse
(9) suicide attempt
(10) vague somatic complaints not explained by physical findings
(11) evasive or embarrassed answers

Physical Examination

(1) physical findings do not match history
(2) suspicious interaction between companion and patient
(3) malnutrition (without illness-related cause)
(4) dehydration (without illness-related cause)
(5) poor personal hygiene
(6) pressure sores
(7) signs of over-, under-, or mismedication
(8) injuries (fractures, burns, head or face injuries, bruises)
(9) evidence of sexual activity in a patient unable to consent or denying sexual activity

Once the suspicion of possible mistreatment or neglect is raised, a comprehensive assessment of the potential abuse situation must be made by a physician, nurse, or social worker, or, preferably, a team of health professionals with special skills in this area. The protocol we have developed for this assessment elicits information in the following areas:

(1) the patient's cognitive status: We use the Blessed Mental Status Test as a screening instrument, although other screening mental status exams, such as the Folstein Mini-Mental State or the Kahn-Goldfarb, would also be appropriate (see Appendices B and C)
(2) the patient's functional status: level of independence in activities of daily living (self care, ambulation, meal preparation, financial management, shopping, housework); presence or absence of help if the patient is dependent in activities of daily living
(3) social support system, utilization of community social services, financial status
(4) patient's quality of life (level of satisfaction, daily activities, personal relationships)
(5) experience of abuse or neglect (physical violence, social isolation, restraint, financial exploitation, withholding of food, medication, or other comforts, oversedation, threats)
(6) interview of caregiver or companion (quality of relationship with patient, evidence of health or mental health problems, drug or alcohol abuse, other severe psychosocial stress, level of frustration with care burden, level of understanding of condition)

In Mr. Washington's case, a number of these areas may be complex and need particular attention if one is to make an accurate assessment and an appropriate intervention. First is the issue of his "competence"; his level of cognitive function will determine the degree to which he is able to participate in decision making and may help clarify the risk of abuse. A cognitively impaired patient may impose a particularly heavy care burden on the caretaker, thus creating a risk for abuse by the caretaker; conversely, an agitated, cognitively impaired caretaker may physically abuse the patient. The actual designation of competence, or lack of it, is a legal determination; however, it is well within the purview of the physician to determine the presence of cognitive impairment by formal mental status testing, possibly with the help of comprehensive neuropsychological testing in appropriate cases. The determination of the patient's ability to participate in decision making, and therefore in discharge planning, is crucial.

The next area that needs special attention is that of Mr. Washington's psychological status, particularly concerning the possibility of a clinical depression. His extreme pain in conjunction with his complaints of diminished appetite and sleep disturbance certainly raise the possibility of depression. The presence of depression would significantly affect the evaluation of both cognitive and psychological status and management of this situation; it may be a significant variable in the stresses placed on Mrs. Washington as the caretaker; it may significantly hinder Mr. Washington's ability to participate in a therapeutic plan and respond to a rehabilitative program, and may even be implicated in the reported episodes of confusion (pseudodementia).

For both, the evaluation of cognitive and psychological status and the collaboration of a psychiatrist and/or neuropsychologist may be helpful and should continue to be encouraged. Given Mr. Washington's probable sense of abandonment at this point, the suggestion must be made carefully, with reassurances concerning the ongoing relationship with the primary care physician. If Mr. Washington continues to refuse, the assessment team of professionals already working with, and familiar to, Mr. Washington must proceed with an assessment in these areas, and may seek advice from a psychiatrist and/or neuropsychologist as they proceed.

Finally, and importantly, the medical management of Mr. Washington's condition must be carefully assessed. Both Mr. Washington's and his wife's understanding of the situation must be elicited, with particular attention given to unstated fears that may be heightening stress in the relationship. For instance, Mr. Washington's somewhat realistic fears of leg amputation may have engendered similar fears in his wife, with an expectation of increasing dependence by her husband and a feeling that she could not cope in that situation. Making these fears explicit could allow planning for eventualities that would offer options for assistance, thereby decreasing the level of fear and resulting stress. The issue of pain and pain medication needs to be clarified, in particular, exactly how the medication is being taken and who is in charge of it. Mr. Washington's ability to regulate his own medication must be assessed, including the impact of his cognitive and psychological status on this function. Since the periods of mental confusion are possibly related to analgesic drugs, the drugs being used must be considered in this light. If Mrs. Washington is in charge of administration of pain medication, her ideas about this role must be explored, given the propensity of caregivers to underutilize analgesics in chronic pain syndromes, and the potentially powerful controlling effect this withholding may produce.

This entire effort at clarification must be seen in the context of the strife that already exists between Mr. and Mrs. Washington. This strife may have devastating effects on the potential for an optimal medical outcome and may seriously hamper attempts at discharge planning. The management team has a lot of work to do in order to arrive at a reasonable level of clarification of all of these issues. The clarification process itself may prove therapeutic, and may obviate the need for legal intervention suggested by both Mr. and Mrs. Washington. If, instead, the clarification yields documentation of abuse, then appropriate intervention efforts can be initiated.

HOWARD WASHINGTON—STUDY QUESTIONS

(1) Detection

    (a)   Is there evidence that abuse has occurred?

    (b)   What is the best way to structure counseling interviews in order to elicit information about abuse? (For example, should family members be interviewed together?)

(2) Assessment

    (a)   Who should the hospital view as the client? How does the answer to this influence assessment and case planning?

    (b)   Is there any indication that there is a pattern of abuse?

    (c)   What questions should be asked to ascertain frequency, severity, and history of abuse? How do the answers to these questions influence case planning?

    (d)   What is the cause of abuse in this case? If the etiology is unclear, what questions should the social worker ask to gain a better understanding of it? Why is this knowledge important?

    (e)   How long has the abuse been going on? If this is unclear, what questions should be asked to ascertain this information? Is there any reason to suspect that stress on the family precipitated the onset of the abuse?

    (f)   What are possible explanations for why Mr. Washington is talking about the abuse now? Why has Mrs. Washington now decided that she does not want to live with her husband any longer?

    (g)   How much information is needed about other members of the family and other support networks in order to help Mr. Washington and Mrs. Washington?

    (h)   What features in Mr. Washington's history should be further investigated to make an accurate health assessment? (For example, depression? Pseudodementia? Medication abuse?)

    (i)   Is the patient competent? How can this be established? How does the answer to this affect case plans?

    (j)   Is it necessary to call in a psychiatric consultant? Why or why not? If yes, how can the physician work with Mr. Washington's resistance to this? If the patient continues to refuse, how should the physician proceed?

(k) Should the physician be concerned that the family strife erupting now may worsen Mr. Washington's health condition? Does this influence the way Mr. Washington should be involved in the discharge planning process?

(l) What is the role of the interdisciplinary team in assessing abuse and deciding case plans?

(3) Interventions

(a) What are possible short-term case plans?

(b) What are possible long-term case plans?

(c) How do the different family members perceive the problem and how does this influence case planning?

(d) What are the hallmarks of successful interventions?

(e) Are there any intervention pitfalls of which workers should be aware?

(f) Does the existence of DRGs influence discharge planning? Why or why not? (Please remember DRG regulations vary from state to state.)

SUMMARY

There is great flexibility and variation in what roles and responsibilities an individual professional will assume when working with elder mistreatment victims. This often depends on organizational policy, the job description, and the individual's interpretation of her or his professional responsibility. The following summarizes the roles and responsibilities of the different professions as discussed in the responses to three case studies. This discussion is not meant to be exhaustive. Each professional may have additional roles and responsibilities not mentioned here.

Nurse: One major responsibility of the nurse is the comprehensive assessment of the patient's health, emotional, and service needs. Implied in this assessment is establishing the competency of the victim, either by administering a Mini-Mental Status Exam or by involving another professional capable of this assessment. In order to assess the patient accurately, the nurse needs to establish a supportive relationship with the victim, have a sensitivity to aging issues, and have the ability to distinguish between normal and pathological aging. The nurse may also need to talk with family members. Finally, the nurse should involve the victim in short- and long-term planning, in order to ensure the victim's active participation and approval of the intervention planned.

Attorney: Criminal and civil laws are often complex and change frequently, making it nearly impossible for nonlawyers to keep abreast of all the laws impacting on victims. Attorneys can provide information about the courts, for example, how to obtain an Order of Protection or provide information on legal interventions (e.g., substituted judgment alternatives and how to establish them).

Victims of elder mistreatment underutilize the criminal justice system for many reasons, one of which is that the victims and professionals often do not acknowledge that a crime has taken place. Attorneys can define abusive behavior in the context of criminal law and can inform victims and professionals how to document and pursue criminal prosecution.

Attorneys working in the criminal and family courts are often knowledgeable of services available through the courts (e.g., drug or alcohol treatment programs for abusers and advocacy and counseling services for victims).

Physician: Physicians need to be knowledgeable of the signs and symptoms of mistreatment in order to recognize it and avoid being susceptible to ageist stereotypes (e.g., older patients always complain). Once detected, physician assessment should include the mental, functional, health, and emotional status of the victim. The physician also needs to have knowledge of the victim's support system, quality of life, and past experience of mistreatment in order to plan effectively for the patient. Family members often want to express their opinions to the physician making the physician pivotal in the investigatory process. The physician should also be able to assess the need for collaboration with other professionals and consult with them as necessary.

Social worker: One major responsibility of the social worker is to provide counseling to the victim. First, the social worker must establish a trusting relationship with the victim and maintain a nonjudgmental attitude. Counseling might best be conducted away from the office, perhaps in the victim's home. Thus the social worker needs to be able to conduct a safety assessment to ensure that home visiting is feasible.

The social worker needs to assess accurately the client's health care, functional, financial, and emotional needs. If the worker lacks the necessary knowledge to do this assessment, he or she should involve the appropriate professionals. Also, the worker should obtain information on the history of the mistreatment and all interventions tried in the past. Usually the worker will need to decide if other family members should be interviewed, and should consider their possible role in the abusive situation before structuring those sessions. One aspect of counseling is to educate the victim about patterns of mistreatment as well as all intervention options available. Finally, the social worker should develop short- and long-term goals, in consultation with the victim, and make appropriate referrals and coordinate other services as necessary.

Obviously, there are overlapping roles. For example, both the nurse and the social worker might do a comprehensive assessment. If a team exists, professionals must define their roles on a case-by-case basis to minimize duplication of effort. When a team does not exist, often a case manager coordinates involved professionals and defines their roles in consultation with them. All professionals need to have well-developed communication skills, not only to interact successfully with the elder victim, but also to have optimal interdisciplinary communication.

Chapter 7

TESTIMONIES

The purpose of this chapter is to provide you with an understanding of the victim's perspective on the problem of elder mistreatment. First-hand accounts by four elder abuse victims are presented. All of these victims are participants in an ongoing support group sponsored by the Victim Services Agency (VSA) of New York City. Direct transcriptions of the support group discussion are presented, although identifying information has been omitted in order to ensure anonymity. Discussions were taped in two interview sessions conducted within a one-month period.

This chapter demonstrates the value of victim support groups. There is a consensus among group members that their most important assistance comes from each other as a result of the support group. In addition, members cite the group as the one essential ingredient that has allowed them to make progress. The verbatim transcriptions in this chapter provide a sense of these group dynamics and underscore the value of such groups. Furthermore, it becomes clear that, although victims have experienced similar situations of abuse, each individual's needs, responses, and ultimate solutions are different. The testimonies that follow reveal, at least in part, how members of the support group help each other arrive at the best resolutions to each individual's problem(s).

This chapter also illustrates some of the concepts discussed in Chapter 4 relating to the different stages through which victims move in order to arrive at a life without violence. In particular, the testimonies presented may help the reader understand the concept of "change over time." Since most of the victims who speak in this chapter have been working on the mistreatment in their lives for several years, they confirm that changes do not occur quickly and that progress usually takes place in incremental steps rather than in rapid advances.

While the discussion provides some insight into the perspectives of mistreatment victims, it is not intended as a profile of the "typical victim." For example, all of the members of the group are white females between the ages of 65 and 72. All live in an urban environment. In addition, all were abused by their children or sons- or daughters-in-law. The chapter is organized into four parts. In the first section, "What Happened," the reader is provided with a sense of each of the four victims' stories, what types of mistreatment took place, and what they were thinking and feeling at the point they decided to seek help. In the second section, "Seeking Help," the victims explain which interventions were helpful and which were not, and they talk about what professionals can do in order to assist victims of elder abuse more effectively. In the third section, "Advice to Victims," members discuss what other victims can do to help themselves. And the last section, "Taking Stock," looks at the changes which have occurred over time in the lives of these group members.

Brief summaries are interspersed to identify key concepts and issues. Questions the authors considered particularly significant are shown in bold type.

WHAT HAPPENED

VICTIM 1: ALICE

INTRVWR: **Alice, why did you seek help?**

ALICE: That's a good question. I don't know. I knew I had to get some help. My daughter was sick, she was in and out of the hospital, and she was giving me a pretty bad time. These things I try to block out of my mind. I want to forget it, I guess.

When I came to VSA, my daughter had already been in the hospital and released. But she had a problem. She wouldn't follow-up after she got out of the hospital. She wouldn't go back for any medication or help. She said she was fine, and she wasn't, and I wasn't able to handle it. I just didn't know who to turn to.

INTRVWR: She wouldn't listen to you?

ALICE: No, she would keep saying to me—"I've got to talk to you, you've got to help me"—but at the same time she would tell me there's nothing the matter with her. She was very confused, which made me confused too, because at times she kept telling me that I had a problem and that I should get help. It went on for a long time and I was beginning to think she was right. Maybe I did have a problem. I did, I guess, in handling this. I was confused myself, you know.

INTRVWR: About how to handle it?

ALICE: Yeah, you get confused. You don't sleep at night wondering what you should do and, you know, trying to figure it out. Are you doing the right thing and all this. And then its very hard to get anybody, you know, to help. Like, when they let her out of the hospital she wasn't capable. She wouldn't go to sign on for any kind of money to help in her life, like welfare.

INTRVWR: Why?

ALICE: She wouldn't do that. She said that she'd never done that.

INTRVWR: She felt that it was beneath her?

ALICE: Beneath her, and she wouldn't do it. And then I had to come up with the money for her. My husband died then and I didn't have a lot of money, but what I had was being used up trying to help her, and I knew it wasn't the right thing to do.

INTRVWR: **What was it that brought you to finally seek help?**

ALICE: I realized that I would have to get her out of there, or I would have to get myself out, because I just could not take it. I was getting no rest and she was pushing me around and it was getting very bad. Now I look back and I wonder how I did it. I couldn't do it again. I was pretty stupid to do it that long. I think as a child she was spoiled and I was always giving her everything she wanted. Maybe that was it. When she wanted money, I would give it to her. She had her own business twice—she started up a beauty parlor twice and she closed it twice. And that was a lot of money down the drain and it didn't bother her.

INTRVWR: So, it sounds like at the point you sought help, you felt like you couldn't take it anymore.

ALICE: I was getting very nervous. I was afraid I would hurt her if I didn't get some help because she was keeping after me so much. Maybe at times I thought that, but I don't think it could have really happened. I just didn't want any more trouble. I wanted to get away from her.

I went first of all to family court. Somebody told me to go there. Well, I went in, there were crowds of people, and I got scared, so I left. And I went out and I saw a senior citizen's center. So, I went in there to see if they could help me. They gave me the number for VSA, so then I came here. And from then on I was able to get a better insight into the whole thing.

INTRVWR: **What kinds of things would your daughter do to you when she was abusive?**

ALICE: Oh, she often slapped me in the face. Yes, if she didn't get what she wanted. And she would scream at me and call me all kinds of names. And at night, she would come into my room and say, "I gotta talk to you, I gotta talk to you." Some nights I got very little sleep.

INTRVWR: You couldn't sleep because you were interrupted?

ALICE: Yes.

INTRVWR: How long had this been going on?

ALICE: It had been about five years. It was going on, you know, but it was getting gradually worse.

INTRVWR: What had happened that helped you realize you needed to do something different than you had for five years?

ALICE: I guess I got to the end of my rope, I just didn't know what to do. I couldn't take it anymore. I knew I felt like just packing up and going away somewhere and then I told myself I was just going to bring my problems with me. So I better get some help and see somebody. I had paid so much money to psychiatrists for my daughter that I couldn't afford to go and see one myself. She was working sometimes, and sometimes she paid for it herself. She would work for maybe three or four months and then she would stop. Those few months she would be fine and then this would come over her again, this depression.

INTRVWR: **What did you do to get your daughter's behavior to conform to your standards?**

ALICE: I never really did. I learned at VSA that I wasn't the only one who had this problem and that there were ways of handling it, you know, that I was allowing her to have too much of her own way.

INTRVWR: Setting limits then?

ALICE: Yeah, I had to set limits, which I learned about here.

INTRVWR: Did that help?

ALICE: Oh, definitely, yes. From then on I was able to handle it better, you know. I had somebody behind me. I knew I could call and talk.

INTRVWR: You weren't alone in it?

ALICE: I wasn't alone, which is the greatest feeling in the world. Before, I was.

INTRVWR: Were you able to make it clear to your daughter, that if she wanted to stay with you, she would have to take her medicines and get follow-up help from the psychiatrist?

ALICE: To a certain extent, but not all the time. She didn't always listen to me. But still, even though she didn't, I had this group to come to and I had somebody to talk to about it when I had a big problem. I can't explain it, but it meant everything—it was night and day to me. It made such a difference that I had somebody to come to.

INTRVWR: **Can you remember the first person to say that you were being mistreated, and that this was the major problem?**

ALICE: Yes. When I came to VSA.

INTRVWR: What was your reaction to that?

ALICE: I was glad to hear that. I knew I wasn't doing the right thing. But I didn't know how to go about it. It's hard to explain but I knew that I wasn't handling it right, but when somebody started to help me I'd go from there. It was great, really.

INTRVWR: How long have you been coming to the group?

ALICE: Since the group started, about three years ago. But I had been coming for individual counseling for about a year before that. I saw the graduate student.

INTRVWR: And was that helpful?

ALICE: Well, she was a very intelligent girl. Really, I can't put my finger on it. But she let me know I had a life of my own and that I should be thinking sometimes more about myself than my daughter.

INTRVWR: Did you ever meet with the student and your daughter?

ALICE: Once she went over to the psychiatric hospital when my daughter was there. There was a group meeting and the student went to that with me.

INTRVWR: It sounds like you have things pretty much under control now, but it also sounds like at times there are still problems.

ALICE: Oh, definitely, yes. But she got married since. She got married a few months ago.

INTRVWR: Is she still living with you?

ALICE: Yes. She's supposed to be looking for an apartment. So far they haven't got one. And her husband is a great help to her. He has helped her enormously. I think they had gone out together for only a few months. A few weeks ago, he had to take her to the hospital. She had a panic attack. He didn't know anything about how to handle this. But she had told him she had been in the hospital. She told him everything before they got married.

INTRVWR: What's a panic attack?

ALICE: Hysteria. She got very hysterical. Everything was wrong and she was crying and someone had to help her and get her to a hospital or do something for her. But you know, I think she was taking diet pills.

INTRVWR: But also you did say that she had a history of problems, psychiatric problems, so I don't know what the underlying problem is. It may not have been the diet pills. Was she taking medication for her psychiatric problems?

ALICE: No, she hadn't been taking her medicine.

INTRVWR: How did she meet her husband?

ALICE: She met him at a discotheque. He's been very helpful to her.

INTRVWR: How does he help?

ALICE: He's 10 years younger than her. He's always telling her how great she is whenever she does the cooking or anything.

INTRVWR: So he helps her like herself.

ALICE: Yes. And he takes her out to eat. He's been a godsend, believe me. If he left her, I don't know what would happen.

INTRVWR: Has she acted negatively toward you since he's been on the scene?

ALICE: A few times she's told me to mind my own business. But she was probably right.

INTRVWR: Has she slapped you?

ALICE: Oh, no, not in front of him. I don't think he would allow it.

INTRVWR: So he's a limit-setter?

ALICE: Yes. A few times he's told her that it isn't right to talk to me the way she does sometimes.

INTRVWR: When was the last time she hit you?

ALICE: It's been a couple of years.

INTRVWR: So it was a while ago.

ALICE: Yes.

INTRVWR: Interesting. So she really responds to people saying, "No. Certain behaviors are not permitted."

ALICE: Yeah. Although I think her husband is the one she listens to more than anybody. She didn't always listen to me. But I think in getting help for myself I can now handle the situation better, and help her too. You work both ways. Because if you don't get help for yourself you can't help someone else. It is impossible.

Summary

Alice was abused physically and psychologically by her daughter, who suffers from a mental illness. It is unclear whether or not Alice's daughter financially exploited her, although Alice's daughter was financially dependent on her. (The daughter refused to seek public assistance, worked only sporadically, and lived with Alice.)

Alice states that the abuse had gone on for the past five years and had gradually gotten worse over the years. As noted in other parts of this book, this is a typical pattern. The first intervention Alice tried was seeking psychiatric help for her daughter. Her initial emphasis was on getting this help for her daughter, and she did not focus on the abuse she suffered at all. This is typical of victims in the reluctance stage. Alice mentions that her daughter accused her of having the problems, and, as is common for victims in reluctance, Alice agreed: "Maybe I did have a problem."

As the abuse worsened, and when she feared that she would begin to harm her daughter, Alice attempted other solutions. She tried to use the family court, but was too scared. This is indicative of victims in the recognition stage: Alice attempted to try something new, motivated by fear, but lacked the confidence, information, and support to be successful. She went to a senior center, which referred her to a victim assistance agency where she received individual and group counseling services. Through these experiences, Alice's isolation was decreased: She learned that others are also abused by family members and received support and guidance in handling the abuse problems. She describes this as the "greatest feeling in the world," knowing that one is not alone.

Alice states that one of the most important things she learned was that she needed to focus on herself, rather than just on her daughter. When she was able to do this, she was able to be much more firm with her daughter and risk losing the relationship she had with her daughter. Still, by the close of the interview, it was clear that Alice had not yet accepted the chronic nature of her daughter's mental illness. (Her daughter did not take her medications and when she had the "panic attack," it was attributed to diet pills rather than to underlying psychiatric problems.) Nor does Alice believe that her daughter is necessarily more responsive to her now and attributes the change to the presence of her son-in-law. This is in spite of the available evidence, that her daughter has not been physically abusive for two and a half years and her son-in-law has been in the picture only a few months.

Alice is someone who has made tremendous progress over the years. She is no longer isolated, she blames herself less, and she understands her options and has tried new solutions. Yet, she does not trust that she would force her daughter out of her home, should that be necessary. All of these features place her solidly in the recognition stage.

VICTIM 2: BERNICE

INTRVWR: **How about you, Bernice? Why did you seek help?**

BERNICE: I have a son who started at the age of 19 with mental illness. He was hospitalized a number of times and classified as a paranoid schizophrenic. He tried to kill himself twice. He was not living at home from age 19 on. He would come to the house and first verbally then physically be abusive to his father and then to me. I remember calling the police and they wouldn't come to the house because they said it was a family problem. And I said, "What are you going to do? Wait until he kills me and then you'll come and pick him up?" I was very upset, to say the least.

Well, needless to say, they didn't come, but we managed to get him out of the house. A couple of times after that he would come to the house. Again we would call the police and this time they came because he hit my husband and had broken his glasses, hit me, was ranting and raving. The first thing they asked him was, "Do you live here?" And he said, "No." And they said, "Well, you have no business here." He said, "This is my house. My parents have $10,000 of mine. I want it." I don't know where he got that figure; it was a nice round figure, I guess. But they took him out, and he was hospitalized again after that.

He spent 13 months at a mental hospital, where he ended up with a broken arm because he got physically violent and in subduing him they broke his arm. I've been to many sessions with the family groups, psychiatry and all of this. And I got absolutely nothing out of it. All it did was make me feel guilty, like it was my fault. And of course to my son, it is my fault. Not his father's, mine.

The last time he came to the house, I called the police. They came, and one of the policemen said that they can't keep coming every time I call. He suggested I get an Order of Protection. They told me I had to go to court, and I didn't realize what an involved process this was. I thought you go in and say you need it and—bingo!—they give you a paper and that's it. But I had to go back twice because at four o'clock they said, "No more today. Come back tomorrow." And, you know, going through that security thing is very degrading.

And when I got up to the floor, there was nobody to tell me what to do. I found it very uncomfortable and very disconcerting. They finally called me in and set a date for a hearing. And I went for the hearing hoping my son wouldn't show up. But he did. And the court officer called my name, and he said, "All right, you just wait." And he called my son and he spoke with him. Then he came over to me and he said that my son was not going to contest it. He told me to sit and wait until they called. And when they did call us into the judge's chambers, the judge gave me the paper and then made a remark which got me very upset. He said, "We have to forgive our bad sons." Because my son was "yes-siring" the judge to death. No matter what, he said, "yes sir." "Do you understand?" "Yes sir." And so on. And I said, "There is more than just a bad son here, your honor. There is much more involved."

And last year my son was arrested for assaulting someone. And with his history, he was sent to jail for three months. Which is something I could never understand. I thought he would go to a psychiatric facility. When he got out of there he kept coming around. He always wanted money. He gets Medicaid and he recently got SSI.

INTRVWR: **So how did you hear about this group?**

BERNICE: Through the courts. After I got the Order of Protection, they sent me down to some office. And, you know, I was in such a state I don't know who I spoke with there, but they gave me VSA's number to call. I had no idea what the support group was about, but I figured I'd gone this far, what could I lose? And I finally came here and I met these ladies and I started coming to this. And I find it's good for me, because I find there are other people in my boat, and when I say something to them they understand and they're not condemning me. Because my friends, who have known my son all his life, will say things like, "How can you do that! He's your son!" I feel it is either me or him. And at this stage of my life, I want it to be me. He's got a long way to go; I don't have that much time.

INTRVWR: **At what point did it occur to you that you had to help yourself?**

BERNICE: After coming here. Because when I first went for the Order of Protection my husband was angry at me. Even though he's the one who called the police, he said, "How can you do that?" And I said, "I can't help it. It's either that or I'm going to go crazy."

And then when I came here I could never talk about any of this without crying. My friends didn't understand. They just didn't. One of them said to me, "Why do you go to that group? Talk to us!" But I said, "Yes, but you don't understand." They still say to me, "How can you do that to your son?"

INTRVWR: And here there is more understanding?

BERNICE: Well, because they've been through it. My son is like a Jekyll-and-Hyde. He can be fantastic sometimes. But you say "no" to him, well, he's a whole different person. And if you talk to him long enough he doesn't make sense, even on his good days. He doesn't remember what he says, he denies saying things that he said, he denies doing things that he's done. And I haven't got a witness to any of this. It got to a point where I was saying, "Maybe I'm imagining a lot of this." Because nobody else is seeing any of this.

INTRVWR: Has your husband been interested at all in joining the group?

BERNICE: No. Not at all. I mean, as far as my husband's concerned, he's just sort of wiped it out of his mind.

ALICE: He can do that?

BERNICE: He may think about it but he won't talk about it. He doesn't want to hear me talk about it.

ALICE: That's what I mean, he actually can't wipe it out of his mind. It's still there, but he doesn't talk about it.

BERNICE: Well, that's very possible.

INTRVWR: **So you deal with the problems directly and your husband has another way.**

BERNICE: Yeah. My husband just ignores it. But the thing is that my son didn't come around when my husband was home. He'd come around when he knew he wasn't home. He'd see that the car wasn't at the house.

INTRVWR: But he did abuse your husband on a couple of occasions.

BERNICE: Yes, yes. But this was before we started calling the police and all of this.

INTRVWR: Your husband would prefer not to do that.

BERNICE: Of course not! Besides being embarrassing, my son was so unstable there for awhile I didn't know what he was going to do. It was fear on my part that made me go through this. And even now, even with the Order of Protection, he goes to church on Sundays and I don't go as often as I used to because he's there. And he walks up the hill with me and always asks me for money and stuff and the first time he did it I said, "I have an Order of Protection, which is to prevent this kind of thing." And he says, "Oh, that. That don't mean a thing."

INTRVWR: So he doesn't take it seriously.

BERNICE: No. Which upsets me too. He's not a stable person.

ALICE: That's why he doesn't take it serious.

BERNICE: I mean, like, the rules are made for everybody but him.

INTRVWR: That's tough to deal with.

BERNICE: Yes. And he's going to be 33 years old and he's a nothing.

Summary

Bernice's adult child has a history of chronic mental illness, which is similar to Alice's situation. Bernice's son does not reside in his parent's home: It appears he drops by, uninvited, and is abusive both physically and psychologically, usually to exploit them financially. Bernice does not deny the seriousness of her son's mental illness, nor does she minimize the seriousness of the abuse, indicative of a victim in the rebuilding stage. Her husband, she claimed, would rather try to ignore the problems than confront them. (When two parents are abused by an adult child, often they are not united on how to handle the problem. It is common for one parent to want to call the police, for example, and the other to want to solve the problems privately. Oftentimes, the parents switch roles midstream: The parent who wanted to solve the problem privately decides to take legal action, and the parent who wanted to call the police decides it really is a private matter after all. This ultimately works toward maintaining the status quo.)

Bernice claimed that fear motivated her to seek help, which is common in many elder abuse situations. She called the police numerous times, and she often felt unprotected by them. Many victims report that the police response is inadequate. Some victims claim that the response time was too slow; others feel abandoned when the police walk away and minimize the seriousness as a "family matter." Some victims claim that when the abuser says, "Don't listen to my mother, she has Alzheimer's," the police ride away, believing the myth that aging and senility are synonymous. Many communities now mandate that the police make an arrest on probable cause of a felony, and train the police on the appropriate response to domestic violence.

Bernice went to court for an order of protection, and she described how complicated, confusing, and intimidating the process was. Many victims share Bernice's view of the court system. Many elder abuse victims have never had a reason to be in a courtroom, other than to serve on jury duty, and facing a judge is frightening. Bernice thought the judge did not understand the seriousness of the abuse when he said, "We must forgive our bad sons." Not only is this an expression of leniency, which the abuser heard, but it blames the victim. Victim disaffection with the court system is partly caused by their feeling degraded and intimidated by it. To increase victim participation in the court system, advocacy programs have been developed in many family and criminal courts to assist victims.

Bernice also tried different counseling programs. She found the elder abuse victim support group to be the most helpful. For the first time, she felt accepted and understood.

VICTIM 3: CAROL

INTRVWR: **How about you, Carol? Why did you seek help?**

CAROL: My son was never abusive to the point of hitting me or anything. But he was abusive in taking my things, my jewelry. I couldn't keep money in the house. It made me feel like I didn't know if I was coming or going. He made me feel very inadequate, like I didn't know what I was doing. If I had 10 dollars and it disappeared, I used to think, "Boy, what did I do with it? It's not there; I must have spent it." Everything was, "I must have done it."

Then he was going with this girl. Her mother had thrown her out of the house and they stayed with me. They took the extra bedroom. When my father passed away, my son was very considerate. They had gotten an apartment. They were living together; this was the third apartment. And it wasn't working and I didn't know why. Now when I look back at it, they must've been using drugs, some kind of drugs.

It was always me. I was always the wrong one. Until they decided to get married. I didn't want them to get married because they weren't right for each other. And I tried so hard not to let it happen, but her stepmother decided that if they wanted to get married, we should make them a wedding. So we made them a wedding. Not a big thing. It was at her father's house; her mother and father are separated. And they had the wedding. They went to live with her father. I don't know what happened, but they were thrown out of his house.

One day they came to my house. They were on a boat and they both fell. He had a fractured foot and she was cut up, and they were in the hospital for medical attention and had no place to go. So I took them in. And from then on it was unbearable. She was abusive to me. I am almost sure she was high on something, I don't know what. One time she was on the phone. I was getting $80 telephone bills and I said, "Listen, you got a mother. Get out of the house and go to your mother. My son can stay with me; you go to your mother's house." No, he wouldn't let her go.

Once she was on the phone long-distance. And I said to her, "I'm sorry!" I took the phone out of her hand and I hung it up. I didn't know she was in that kind of a mood. I have rheumatoid arthritis and I'm not very steady on my feet. She just turned around and took me by the shoulders and threw me against the wall. My son heard something going on, so he ran into the kitchen. He almost killed her. "Don't you ever touch my mother! Don't you ever do this." Not that he was that good, but don't somebody else do it to his mother. And I said to them, "This is the last straw. You've got to get out." I was really scared of them. I really was.

And it got worse. She went through my drawers, she took my credit cards, went to Macy's. She was caught in Macy's using my credit card. She went to jail and got out. I didn't know where to turn. Her parents wouldn't do anything about it. They wouldn't take her, they didn't want to hear about her, they didn't want to hear about my son.

INTRVWR: What do you think of the fact that they didn't want their daughter back?

CAROL: I don't know what to think about it, truthfully. I honestly don't. Because it was their child and their problem and I didn't want it. I had enough with my child and my problems, I didn't want their problems.

He used to have a very good job and she used to go on the job and the boss didn't like it, and he got fired. And she had a million jobs and couldn't hold on to them. Whatever.

One day I was watching television and I heard something about VSA and I don't know, it stuck in my mind. I didn't do anything right away. But one day she wanted the key to my mailbox and I wouldn't give it to her. Most of the mail was mine! And I was getting checks and things like that, and I wouldn't give her my key. And she threatened me. I said, "If you don't get out of my house right now I'm calling the cops." I had called the cops before and the cops came. You know what they told me? "Are you sure you want to do this to your child before Christmas? You want to put him out on the street before Christmas?" And I said to them, "If I hadn't wanted him on the street before Christmas I wouldn't've called you." Think about it. And they said, "You know, these things straighten out." Here I am, crying, not wanting to be in the same room as them. And I felt sorry for the police, they didn't know what to do. I don't want cops like that on the force. My money that goes to taxes, which may not be much, but it's what I can pay, I need that protection. These cops should be made aware of what's going on.

INTRVWR: **Did you talk to other professionals?**

CAROL: I spoke with my doctor and he said to me, "You know, you have family in Florida. Wouldn't it be a good idea to pick yourself up and get away?" That's after working my whole life. I have to run? I should have listened. He was a smart man. I should've listened. Had I listened, maybe they would have followed me, but maybe they wouldn't have. But I didn't. I felt, "Why should I be moving to Florida?" And I was very angry and I was very frustrated because all my friends said, "Maybe you're not doing something right." It always had to be me. It always wound up me. I was the one doing something wrong.

Summary

Carol suffered psychological and financial abuse by her son, and was also abused physically, financially, and psychologically by her daughter-in-law. Carol believes her son and daughter-in-law to be drug users, and makes a connection between the drug use and their abusive behavior.

Carol's son and daughter-in-law resided with her frequently, although they also were able, at times, to maintain their own apartment. There is mention that they lived with the daughter-in-law's father and then her mother, but were thrown out. Carol never found out why, and did not consider the possibility that they may have been abusive to the daughter-in-law's parents. Although Carol did not want to take on her daughter-in-law's problems, she did not mention that perhaps the daughter-in-law's parents did not want the problem either. Carol simply states, "It was their child and their problem, and I didn't want it." In regard to denial, Carol fluctuated between the reluctance and the recognition stages. On the one hand, she acknowledged that her son was mistreating her. On the other hand, she did not seem to think that her daughter-in-law's parents had the right to disassociate themselves from whatever problems their daughter caused. Carol held herself to the same standard, believing that, in order to be a "good" parent, she was responsible for her son's welfare. Thus she did not hold her son responsible for his own behavior.

Carol tried several ways of changing the situation. She called the police, and had a similar experience as Bernice: The police blamed her, asking her how she could throw them out before Christmas, and were not protective. A doctor suggested she move to Florida. Carol considered this an option that might have helped her, but she did not want to give up her home and familiar surroundings. She also felt angry and frustrated that she was the one expected to change her life, feelings many victims have. Finally, similar to Bernice, she felt misunderstood by her friends, and did not feel supported by them.

VICTIM 4: DOLORES

INTRVWR: **Dolores, why did you seek help?**

DOLORES: Well, I bought a house with my daughter and son-in-law. We were all going to live together. But it seemed they had plotted that once I was in the house they wanted me out of the house. I put my daughter's name on the deed, which was the wrong thing to do. Once the name was on the deed they wanted me out.

Her father was very sick, in a wheelchair, but they didn't care. They would just start arguments over anything. And the next thing was, her husband slapped me and he said, "Well, there's no witnesses and you can't do anything about it." So I called the police. And the police came but said it was a family argument so they went away. So I called my son and I told him. He said, "If they come near you at all or threaten you in any way, just keep calling the police." And so, well, a few weeks later they started arguing with me again. They wanted me out of the house and meanwhile I had paid for this whole thing.

INTRVWR: It was your money that bought the house?

DOLORES: Everything. The whole thing. And so the next thing, the arguments started again, and he hit me worse. I called the cops again and again, and they said they couldn't do anything because it was a family argument. Away the police went.

Well, it went on for a few more weeks. My husband had to be fed and everything. He had so many strokes he didn't realize what was going on. I had bought this house because my daughter said that she would live with us and help me with him. Well, anyway, an argument started and I went to call the police. My son-in-law went after me and picked me up and threw me in the air. I came flying down and I hit the coffee table. My foot got cut, and it was bleeding a lot. Then he grabbed me by the throat and choked me. Finally, I got away from him and I ran down the corner and I called the police. I stood outside until the police car came.

But I still didn't know what to do. Anyway, being that it was Christmas, I think, the police did not want to be bothered and so they said, "Lady, the only thing you can do with him is get a court order." I didn't know anything about a court order. I said I also didn't know who I could leave my husband with. They kept saying that getting a court order was the only thing I could do. Well, anyway, my son-in-law must have gotten afraid because that night he packed up, and my daughter packed up with him, and off they went somewhere.

My husband always sat looking at the TV. Well, on the TV came the telephone number of a local senior center. I called them up and explained to them what had happened and said I have to get a court order but I didn't know how to do it. I told them I was stuck here in a new home where I didn't even know what was around the corner. So, the woman said that she would come over to talk with me. That was on a Monday. She came over and she said that I could go back with her to the senior center, which had a facility for sleeping. She told me that I shouldn't stay at home because they might come back. But my husband would not go. So she told me to change all of my locks on the door, and I did.

She came back to visit me again, from the senior center, and my husband had another stroke. I had to call the ambulance and have him taken to the hospital. While he was in the hospital, the woman from the senior center suggested I come see her. I went down there and she asked me why I wouldn't stay there, being that the hospital where my husband was was only a block away. And I said, "Well, I have this house, and I have all these lawyers trying to get my daughter off the deed."

So we went through three different lawyers and they all knew they couldn't get her off the deed but they were stringing me along. Anyway, my husband came home from the hospital, but a few weeks later he had another stroke and had to go to the hospital again. Meanwhile, I had put the house up for sale. My son said, "Look, you went to three lawyers and you are never going to get her off the deed. Sell the house, give her what she wants, get rid of her and get out of there." So, I put the house up for sale.

My husband was in the hospital and I told the hospital staff that my daughter was not to visit him. The woman from the senior center told me about VSA and I came here. VSA helped me get the court order. Then I had to serve my daughter and son-in-law a summons. I didn't know where they were living. But my counselor from VSA and two policemen went with me to my son-in-law's job and I gave him the summons. He was screaming all over the place, screaming all over the street and everything else.

My husband was still in the hospital. He was there eight and a half months. Within that time, I sold the house and put all of my stuff into storage because I didn't have a new apartment yet. I was still in contact with the senior center and they told me that I could pay them $400 per month for a room there and could walk back and forth to the hospital to visit my husband. So I did that. And then they told me to come to meetings at VSA, which I did. Then I had to appear in court to get the court order, and my son-in-law had to appear. He was there with my daughter. My VSA counselor came with me. I got the court order. Then I had to go to the closing of the house. Of course my daughter was there and she took half my money and off she went and I never spoke to her since.

INTRVWR: You mean she got half the money that you made from the sale of the house?

DOLORES: Yep! And then it took almost a year for me to get the new apartment I live in now. My VSA counselor worked hard helping me get that apartment. It wasn't easy. I lived at the senior center facility the whole time I was waiting for the apartment to come through.

INTRVWR: And now you feel settled?

DOLORES: Yes. And as far as I'm concerned, she no longer exists.

INTRVWR: **What was your relationship with your daughter like before all of this happened?**

DOLORES: Oh, she was very nice, but evidently she never told me what her husband was like. I never found out what he was like until I hired a lawyer from around the corner. He was from the area and he knew my son-in-law. And my lawyer told me. So then I found out a lot of things living there.

ALICE: All that time you never knew?

DOLORES: Never, never, never.

INTRVWR: How long were they married?

DOLORES: Twenty-five years!

INTRVWR: So he was the perfect son-in-law for 25 years?

DOLORES: Outwardly, but how would I know what he was like inside?

INTRVWR: You included your daughter's name on the deed out of maternal love?

DOLORES: Well, she said, "Why don't you get a house and I'll take care of it with you and this way you can go out in the car, you won't be stuck by yourself taking care of Dad." I figured my son had a house, so why not help my daughter out? But it didn't work out like that because once I was in the house they wanted me out.

INTRVWR: Was the last time you saw your daughter at the closing?

DOLORES: That's it. My husband died after that.

INTRVWR: Did your daughter and her husband go to the funeral?

DOLORES: No way. I wouldn't've allowed her in.

INTRVWR: Has she called her brother?

DOLORES: He would never talk with her again, for the rest of his life.

INTRVWR: **It sounds like you get support from your son. Has that support helped you?**

DOLORES: Oh, yes. He would never talk with her again. Nobody on my side of the family would ever talk with her again. Never. And it helps knowing they agree with me.

INTRVWR: Does your daughter have any children?

DOLORES: Yes, she does.

INTRVWR: So the children were living with you in the house, too?

DOLORES: One was.

INTRVWR: Do you hear from them at all?

DOLORES: No, and I don't want any part of them.

INTRVWR: It must have been very painful.

DOLORES: It was better it was done this way. I don't want to have anything to do with her anymore.

INTRVWR: And there were a lot of losses during that time. Your husband, your daughter.

DOLORES: I lost the house, I lost everything. I lost a lot of my money. I lost everything. But at least I have my sanity.

Summary

Dolores trusted her daughter and son-in-law completely when she agreed to purchase a house, place her daughter on the deed, and live together with them. Shortly after moving in, her son-in-law became psychologically and physically abusive. She realized that both her daughter and son-in-law were motivated by greed: They wanted to take ownership of the house. It did not take long for Dolores to call the police. When they were not helpful, she turned to her son. She was incredibly resourceful. She called a senior center after seeing an advertisement on television. And later, on the advice and help from a social service agency, she sought help from the courts.

She accepted the seriousness of the situation from the beginning and was not ambivalent about following through on options available to her. This is indicative of a victim in the rebuilding stage. All of Dolores's thoughts and actions were directed at ending the mistreatment.

Dolores talked about what she lost during this time. She lost the house and only recovered half of her investment. She ceased contact with her daughter, son-in-law, and grandchildren. She was incredibly inconvenienced and displaced when she sold the house, having to live at a temporary housing facility and put all her possessions in storage. During this time, her husband was dying in the hospital. But she is quite clear that these losses were preferable to living with the abuse, or, as Dolores claimed, to losing her sanity.

In the following three sections, the INTRVWR is directing questions at the entire group, rather than at individual group members.

SEEKING HELP

INTRVWR: **Looking back, what interventions were helpful?**

ALICE: I was told by my VSA counselor, a graduate student, that I had to think more about myself and have my own life. Not to worry so much about my daughter and to try to get my own life together. At the time, I thought that if I thought more about myself that would be selfish, but as time went on I knew that it was right.

INTRVWR: Do you think that you were just not ready to hear that advice at that time?

ALICE: Probably. I guess I just had nobody to turn to. My family didn't understand. My daughter was always very nice when speaking with my family. And they wouldn't believe that she could be abusive to me. They wouldn't understand so I had to go somewhere. I went to church and I talked with the priest, and he told me he didn't perform miracles. You see, I couldn't think straight. But coming here helped and, little by little, I could think more about myself.

INTRVWR: So the change happened over time. What helped you hear the graduate student's message?

ALICE: Just by thinking it over on my own when I left the individual counseling and support group sessions. I said to myself, "I must think about this." Overnight I didn't do it. I had to work on it.

BERNICE: Helpful is this group, as far as I'm concerned.

ALICE: We understand each other.

Summary

Beginning to think about oneself is a hallmark of healing. Alice states that before she went into counseling, she was unable to give to herself. This is common for victims in the reluctance stage. As you recall from Chapter 4, the victim in this stage believes the only person worthy of their attention and concern is the abuser, denying even their own need for attention.

The abuser, besides demanding attention, persistently chips away at the victim's positive self-concept. This helps create the low self-acceptance the victim experiences. Alice was able to redirect attention—

once reserved only for her daughter—toward herself, after developing a trusting relationship with her counselor and support group members.

BERNICE: And the courts still aren't helpful. If I want to renew my Order of Protection, I have to go through the whole thing all over again. They call this a "permanent Order of Protection," but its only good for a year. So if I want it renewed, I have to go through this whole process all over again, which is the kind of thing I don't look forward to.

CAROL: It is the pits! Believe me.

BERNICE: The last time I was there, they had, over the intercom, a public announcement: There was a man in the building with a gun. And another thing, at one o'clock, everyone has to leave the building. And you come back at two o'clock and you stand on line again and go through the whole procedure of going through security before you get back upstairs. It's crazy.

INTRVWR: **When you spoke with someone like a social worker, or talked with your doctor—before the group—did anybody do or say anything helpful?**

BERNICE: There was nothing anybody did. When I spoke with our clergyman, he said he wasn't trained to handle this kind of thing. When I spoke with my doctor, he put me in a group that had people in it that had problems with little children. There was even a couple with sexual problems.

INTRVWR: Who referred you there?

BERNICE: My fellow workers. My son was in the hospital, and they had the family sessions which we went to. I was still working at the time. I worked at the same hospital where my son was admitted. There was one session I could not make. I called down and I told them that I wasn't going to be able to make it. My boss was going away and I had to do some things. I want you to know that the social worker was so abusive to me. She said, "Don't you realize how important this is?" I said, "Not having a job is important too." I mean, I was going faithfully, and yet she was accusing me of not caring because I was missing the one session. So, I really did not have too much faith in social workers. I hate psychiatrists, too.

A lot of people say to me, "Maybe your son was on drugs." Well, he wasn't living at home, I don't know, maybe he was. But one psychiatrist said—this was a friend's brother—"Some people are born with this and it doesn't show up until their late teens or sometimes even into middle life." I don't know whether it's true or if he was just saying it because he knew she'd tell me and I would feel better. It doesn't matter what the cause was, as far as I'm concerned. The fact is, there is something wrong with him. And that's another thing. My friends say, "He's sick. How can you do this to him?"

ALICE: He's sick, so he should be in the hospital.

BERNICE: That's how I feel about it. I personally feel it isn't safe that he's roaming the streets.

ALICE: He should be in the hospital.

BERNICE: Not only for my safety.

CAROL: But I got no help from anybody. Nobody understood. The court, the lawyers, doctors that I went to. Maybe I wasn't tough. I don't know. Maybe I was so confused that I wasn't giving the right kind of a picture to the people trying to help. I don't know. But I didn't get any help and everybody told me something else. The cops told me one thing, the lawyers told me another thing. Mixed messages. Nobody told me the same thing.

Summary

Attempts were made by the INTRVWR to elicit positive statements from the victims on helpful interventions. As evident from the above, there is a general dissatisfaction with approaches offered, although there is an acknowledgment that some of the gestures were meant well.

CAROL: If I asked questions or I went to people for help, everything they told me was so confused. It didn't make sense to me. Everybody was giving advice but it was all negative advice. Nobody said do something positive.

INTRVWR: Like?

CAROL: The only thing I really could have done positive at the time was think about myself, which I didn't.

INTRVWR: **What advice can you give to professionals so they can better assist victims?**

DOLORES: To listen.

ALICE: To listen.

CAROL: To listen and know what we're saying and how we feel. And they don't want to hear.

INTRVWR: Why do you think they don't want to hear?

CAROL: They don't care.

BERNICE: They don't know what to do.

CAROL: Maybe they don't know how to handle this. They haven't been trained in this.

ALICE: If they really did care and were interested, they would find a way to handle it.

INTRVWR: What would they be able to do? Listening was one thing.

BERNICE: Not giving bad advice would be one thing.

CAROL: I think it would be good if they came to the support group.

DOLORES: And find out.

ALICE: The policemen, they didn't know until the VSA counselor went to the police stations and told them directly. She went down to the precinct and she helped there a lot. She explained my situation to them.

CAROL: What happened with people who are alcoholics? For years they went to doctors, they went to psychiatrists, they went all over. There were no answers. Until one man who was an alcoholic started AA. The only people who can help you are the people who have gone through this. No doctor understands it. No lawyer understands it. No social worker understands it.

ALICE: No priest.

CAROL: I haven't been beaten up but do you know anyone who speaks to his parents by saying, "You don't know anything. You're stupid. Why are you my parents? Look at the way I'm living; you're keeping me down."

INTRVWR: Verbal abuse.

CAROL: All right. And most doctors don't consider that abuse.

INTRVWR: So doctors need to know what abuse is.

CAROL: They need to learn because abuse victims go through this.

INTRVWR: So in order to be of any help professionals need to learn what the phenomenon is. Education is one way. And you want them to listen and to care.

CAROL: A lot of them don't even know that these support groups are here.

DOLORES: They don't even know what's going on.

CAROL: And they're not even interested in finding out.

Summary

The victims described the services most influential in helping them achieve a life without abuse. This included participation in the support group, advocacy with the police, and being referred to appropriate sources. The victims also discussed those characteristics most helpful in responding to the needs of elder mistreatment victims. This included strong listening skills and knowledge about the phenomenon of elder abuse and of how to help. Perhaps most important was the ability to bring to the helping relationship a sense of interest and commitment.

Finally, the victims implied that there is an existential quality to being abused that only those experiencing it could fathom. They suggest that professionals should attend support group sessions to gain a fuller appreciation of their lives.

INTRVWR: **Have friends or relatives given you helpful advice?**

CAROL: I have a friend who is a doctor and you know what advice he gave? He said, "The best thing you could do is to cut him out of your life." Maybe the advice was good.

ALICE: But how could you do that?

CAROL: They don't tell you how to do it. I don't think they would do it. I couldn't cut my kid out of my life.

DOLORES: A lawyer told me to do it. To cut her out and get on with my life.

ALICE: But she doesn't bother you anymore.

DOLORES: Well, she knew she couldn't.

ALICE: Yeah.

INTRVWR: **If a person advises you to cut someone out, is that possible to do?**

ALICE: They don't tell you how to do it.

DOLORES: You have to make up your own mind. Nobody can tell you how, or this or that. You just have to make up your mind and do it, and that's it, you gotta stay with it and stop feeling guilty.

ALICE: There are different cases, Dolores.

CAROL: My own brother says to me, "Get rid of him."

BERNICE: It's easy to say, but how do you do it?

CAROL: Do you want to do it? Can you do it? Nobody asks those questions.

ALICE: Sometimes you can. Dolores's daughter was married to the abuser and she has kept away and hasn't come back to bother her.

DOLORES: She knows she can't come back.

ALICE: She hasn't tried it, let's put it that way.

DOLORES: Well, she knows she can't.

ALICE: Some of them don't know and they try.

DOLORES: Well, she knows.

CAROL: But I'm not happy with that. I want my son. He's the only child I have. He's all I got. I don't have any other family.

ALICE: You want to stay in touch with him.

CAROL: Yes. I don't want the pain. My son is in jail.

DOLORES: But if he came out and threatened to kill you, you'd think a different way.

CAROL: Wait a minute. You're putting it back to where you are. Your case is different. I don't want what you did. Every circumstance is different. I don't want to lose my child. I want my child. I just want to find a way. And I may never find it. I know that. It's very frustrating. And I can't expect a doctor or a social worker to give me an answer. But what most of us do expect is understanding, a little compassion, maybe a word that will lead to a little light. That's all we ask. And if you can't find that anywhere, from people who are supposed to give it to you, then you feel no hope. Then you feel frustrated. Then you blame yourself.

INTRVWR: **Is this a place where each person is helped to come to solutions best for the individual?**

DOLORES: Yes.

CAROL: Yes. Because all the cases aren't the same, and we talk about different things and don't always agree. There are a couple of points during the sessions that something is said which somehow clears a little of the muckiness.

INTRVWR: Do people remember helpful things that have been said, certain phrases that have stuck?

CAROL: "Make myself strong and the abuse won't happen." It hasn't helped because I haven't been able to make myself strong. But that doesn't mean that the words aren't right.

INTRVWR: Make yourself strong. Physically, emotionally, or both?

CAROL: Emotionally. Physically there is very little you can do about it. And we don't get advice on how to get strong when we go to psychiatrists. We don't get that when we go to a doctor.

ALICE: Right.

INTRVWR: **It seems to me that you each have had similar experiences, yet you have found different solutions. What do you think accounts for the different solutions?**

DOLORES: I've never been through anything like this in my life. He could have killed me.

INTRVWR: So it was all of a sudden, out of the blue?

DOLORES: Well, he knew my husband was on his way out. So he probably wanted me to have a heart attack and then the house would be his.

ALICE: Well, if my son-in-law abused me the way hers did, I definitely would have done something drastic. He wouldn't be living with me.

INTRVWR: You think it is different when your child is the one who is abusing?

ALICE: Oh, yes. And Dolores was badly hurt. Weren't you?

DOLORES: Oh, I was badly hurt. I mean, he could have killed me.

ALICE: That was scary.

INTRVWR: Did your daughter ever try to talk to you about it or show any kind of protection towards you? When her husband was violent, did she try to help you?

DOLORES: No, nothing. So that's how I knew it was plotted.

INTRVWR: Do you think it made any difference that you have two children? Your daughter is out of your life but you still have a supportive son. Has that helped you keep your daughter out of your life?

DOLORES: No.

ALICE: There is something to that.

INTRVWR: Alice, you think there is something to this, but Dolores, you don't?

DOLORES: After what she did it would not matter.

INTRVWR: Carol, what do you think?

CAROL: I can understand Dolores's view and I think what she did was right for her. She knows I'm for her. But those circumstances did not happen to me. And I only have one child.

INTRVWR: So you think the number of children you have makes a difference in the way a person handles the abuse?

CAROL: I don't know, I don't know. Wrong is wrong. If my son had hit me instead of my daughter-in-law, I wouldn't feel any better towards him because he is my son. That's why I said I don't know. If somebody is punishing you no matter who it is, you don't want to be punished.

INTRVWR: Whoever it is.

CAROL: Right. I think Dolores had the right to do whatever was best for her.

INTRVWR: And you still think you did the right thing?

DOLORES: Absolutely.

INTRVWR: How have you changed in the way you relate to others?

BERNICE: My very dear friends to this day cannot understand how I could have done what I did as far as my son is concerned. They just say they can't understand it because they remember him from when he was a little boy. He was different then. The only place I can come to where people understand is here at the group, because they have all been through the same kind of thing. My friends made me feel like I was the ogre, I'm the bad guy.

INTRVWR: Do you then look at them less as friends?

BERNICE: Not really. But I feel I can't talk to them about this, because they just don't see it and they don't believe it.

Summary

A common declaration made to victims from professionals, friends, and relatives is, "Cut the abuser out of your life." There is a range of responses to this advice, from successfully separating to deciding not to.

Those victims still wanting contact with the abusing relatives state that the desire to separate correlates with the involvement of nonabusing children in the victim's life. They also maintain that the ease of separation correlates with abuser characteristics. For example, Alice points out that Dolores's daughter avoids contact with her, thereby making the decision to separate a nonissue.

Dolores, a victim not wanting contact with the abuser, disagrees with this view. She postulates that separation is contingent on victim characteristics, that is, unwavering commitment to the separation. This involves sending a strong message to the abuser that he or she is not to make contact for any reason, ever.

Bernice contends that successful separation depends on a combination of victim and abuser characteristics—victim commitment to separation and abuser adherence to the limits set. She gives as an example her firm effort to separate, manifested by obtaining an Order of Protection, which was sabotaged by her son's disregard of it. Workers should note that certain advice, such as, "Cut the abuser out of your life," might be reasonable in some cases, but permanent separation is only a true option for victims in the rebuilding stage. Even then abusers might come around and mistreat the victims.

INTRVWR: **What's been most helpful about coming to the support group?**

ALICE: I used to think I was the only one who has this problem.

CAROL: Or, why did it happen to me?

ALICE: I remember the graduate student said I needed to think more about myself, not to worry so much about my daughter. Which is important. I was worrying too much about my daughter. Sometimes I think you get more respect when you stand up for yourself.

CAROL: I don't think that because someone goes to a professional school they have an answer for me. But, if you listen to me, and even if the advice you give is wrong, the fact that I spent 20 minutes talking to you, and you listened and showed compassion, then that helps me tremendously.

ADVICE TO VICTIMS

INTRVWR: **So how do you give more to yourself?**

BERNICE: Well, you don't learn how to do that until you come to a group like this. I was confused, I didn't listen to anybody. My ears were closed. I didn't know if I was coming or going. When I joined this group, the first time I sat down here and heard the women speaking, I didn't know what it was. Maybe because they had the same kind of problem that I did. Each case was different, of course. But we were all under stress, we were all unsure of ourselves. We didn't know where we belonged. Whether we were doing the right thing or not. Somehow it just jelled. I don't know how.

INTRVWR: You just began to share.

ALICE: I think by letting go, by letting go of my daughter more and thinking more of myself.

CAROL: Why aren't there more people in our group?

INTRVWR: There may be several reasons, one being that not everyone being abused is ready to join a group. Think of your own situation. Think of yourself five years ago.

ALICE: We were afraid to come.

INTRVWR: **How can a person get ready to join a group? What advice can you give to victims?**

BERNICE: The first thing you have to do is admit that you are a victim and not try to hide it from anyone. Because of the shame that comes from being a victim, it's hard to accept.

INTRVWR: **How do you know when you're a victim? What are the signs?**

BERNICE: Well, my son was physically abusive.

INTRVWR: What did he do?

BERNICE: He hit me.

INTRVWR: With his hands?

BERNICE: Oh, yeah. But not only me. My husband, too. And verbally abusive.

INTRVWR: What would he say?

BERNICE: Things like threatening to kill me and wanting money.

INTRVWR: These are some of the signs that you would say to people: "If this is happening to you, consider yourself a victim"?

BERNICE: The first thing that did it for me was being hit. This is not what I'm used to. And I thought there had to be something wrong here. And my son had a history, too. He had a history of mental illness and was in and out of mental hospitals for awhile. Actually, 13, 14 years. Now he's in trouble again. Nothing to do with me but he tried to rob a rectory. And I believe that the priest is going to have him prosecuted. But he can't find him. I don't know where he is.

INTRVWR: **What are some things you'd like to say to victims of elder abuse?**

CAROL: Well, first I would say they need to realize they are a victim.

INTRVWR: Okay. So, first of all, accept the fact that abuse is happening. What next?

DOLORES: Seek help.

INTRVWR: From whom?

DOLORES: Anyone that you can.

BERNICE: Anyone who listens.

INTRVWR: Okay. What else can a victim do to help him- or herself?

ALICE: I've been going out more and socializing more. I have to do something for myself. I can't just concentrate on my daughter's problems. If that's the way she wants to live, then let her live that way.

INTRVWR: There is more to your life.

ALICE: Yeah. There is more. I socialize more. It's helped me let go of thinking about her problems. When I go out I think less about her problems.

INTRVWR: That makes sense. So what you've been doing is thinking about other things, doing other things.

ALICE: Yes. Keep yourself busy. But its very difficult, because I can go right back again to my old ways.

BERNICE: I've been doing volunteer work at a hospital and I do some typing for an attorney, and then, of course, I have the housework and my husband. Fortunately, he does the shopping so that I don't have to worry about that. And I just keep myself busy and try not to think about my son at all.

INTRVWR: So you try to distract yourself?

BERNICE: The least thing I think about.

INTRVWR: You try to focus on it less and less.

BERNICE: Yes.

INTRVWR: And, Dolores, what do you do with your time?

DOLORES: I go out.

CAROL: I think I have learned to accept myself more. I always took the blame, and still do sometimes, for everything. I am trying to let go of that.

INTRVWR: Have the quality of your relationships changed after this experience of being a victim?

ALICE: I had to learn to trust people.

Summary

The above discussion highlights the value of the elder abuse victim support group. While acknowledging the differences in each situation, the members find comfort in knowing that they share a fundamental similarity—a loved one abused them. Having felt misunderstood by professionals, relatives, and friends, there is solace in finally finding support from peers.

The group provides an opportunity to build new relationships and offers support as each member searches for her own solutions.

These members realize that there are victims in their vicinity who are not ready to join the group. Interestingly, the reasons they provide for victims not wanting to join yet (e.g., "not ready," "shame," "not acknowledging the abuse") are characteristics describing victims in the reluctance stage.

They offer advice to other victims who may not be ready to join a group. First, people being abused need to identify themselves as victims by learning the signs of mistreatment. To aid in this revelation, people need to think about barriers to self-detection, including shame or fear of being judged harshly by outsiders. Once a person admits to being a victim, he or she should "seek help" from "anyone who will listen." This may take time, because, having been betrayed by a loved one, many victims need to learn how to trust again. Then, the victims prescribe redirecting focus away from the abuse and the abuser and toward oneself (e.g., seeking new contacts and interests).

TAKING STOCK

INTRVWR: **A lot of people are scared to admit that they have a problem because they fear the changes they might have to make if the abuse problem is looked at directly. There is fear of the unknown. Has your life changed in positive ways since you have looked at the abuse problem directly?**

ALICE: I learned to respect myself more and I now know I deserve better. And that is what helped me make changes in my life. I said, I don't deserve this. She shouldn't abuse me. So it made me do some of the things I had to do.

INTRVWR: So the positive thing is that you like yourself more and you protect yourself more?

ALICE: Yes.

INTRVWR: How about other people?

CAROL: It made me feel stronger. It made me feel that I can put certain restrictions on my son without feeling guilty. And I know in my mind it's not my fault. But it doesn't always work. You're always looking back to see if there is something that you're guilty of like not noticing things, why it happens to you. And it is hard to put together. No matter how hard you try you can't get away from all the suffering.

INTRVWR: It's a constant struggle?

CAROL: Always. No matter what. You're afraid that if a month goes by and nothing bad happens, that—uh oh—it's going to happen next month. It's always there and it's a horrible way to live. And most victims have these feelings and nobody wants to be hurt. And sometimes I still feel guilty.

DOLORES: I think I don't have any reason to feel guilty. They did it, I didn't.

CAROL: We all feel that way, but for some people it's easier to be strong than for others. We're all made differently. But we all can get strong by being together. We had a lot of help from the VSA counselors and volunteers.

INTRVWR: It sounds like its been an evolution.

CAROL: The support group is what I call "help." It gives us a place—I'm not kidding—it gives us a place where we belong. We don't have to worry when we feel like screaming or when we feel like crying or what we say to each other, because we're there for each other.

INTRVWR: That sounds like positive results. It's not everyone who can say that they can talk to others with that degree of intimacy and be treated with respect. Have your views of parenting changed?

BERNICE: Yeah. Well, if I had to do it all over again, sometimes I wonder if I would. I ask myself, "Was it worth it?" I think a lot of us in my generation, when the new permissive education was coming in, we were, at least I was, trying to raise my kids the old-fashioned way, the way my parents did. It was pretty hard to fight television and peer pressure and the new methods of education, and still keep sanity in my family, without arguing with my husband. I think the kids have a much harder time now than we had.

CAROL: I wouldn't want to be a kid growing up today.

DOLORES: I have a great son. My daughter was great until... I don't know whatever happened to her. I guess it was the husband. Maybe she was married to him so long it rubbed off on her. But when she was growing up, she was fine. So I don't know if my views on parenting have changed.

ALICE: I don't think I did anything wrong. I don't blame myself. Maybe I spoiled her a little bit. I gave her maybe more than I should have. Her father died when she was a teenager and she was very upset. So maybe I tried to make up for that and spoiled her a little bit.

The one thing I don't like about this group is the word *victim*. I can't stand it.

BERNICE: None of us can. I don't want to say I'm a victim.

CAROL: "Elder abuse" doesn't sound so great either. It's like, "Oh boy, has it come to this?"

INTRVWR: What don't you like about the word *victim?*

ALICE: It's hard for me to say that I'm going to a victims' group. I don't say it. I say, I'm going to a group.

CAROL: I say that I'm going to a support group.

INTRVWR: What is it about the word *victim?*

ALICE: A victim is never a winner. Victims are losers.

INTRVWR: A victim implies vulnerability.

ALICE: Right.

INTRVWR: What would you prefer the group be called?

CAROL: Support group. Support group for old ladies. (laughter)

INTRVWR: When you first came to VSA did you feel like a victim?

DOLORES: I feel less like a victim than I did then.

ALICE: I guess when I first came I felt like a victim, but I didn't realize it.

BERNICE: Something terrible was happening and I couldn't take it anymore.

INTRVWR: If you were to advertise the group, what would you call it?

ALICE: Support group for victimized people.

CAROL: But people being abused don't feel like it's in the past, like we do, until they go to these groups and understand themselves.

Summary

The victims reflect on the positive changes in their lives. The consensus is that the term *victim* does not respect or credit the tremendous distance they have traveled. It implies vulnerability and perpetuates the feeling of being a loser in a world of winners. Yet it is hard for the members to agree on a word that accurately reflects where all victims stand in addressing their abuse. Although the victimization experience for them is more a part of the past than the present, they know full well that others still suffer every day.

They are able to make decisions now that promote personal safety. Because they experience less guilt, have more self-respect and have developed a reservoir of emotional strength, and have found some basis of support, they are able to set limits with the abusive relative. At the same time, they are aware that their personal struggles continue and that there is still work left to be done.

Chapter 8

FUTURE DIRECTIONS

It has been less than 10 years since the first research on elder mistreatment was conducted, since the first congressional hearings were held, and since the nation first became aware of this phenomenon through increased media coverage. In that short period of time, over 40 states have passed mandatory reporting laws regarding elder mistreatment. There have been several national conferences focused on the topic, and there has been a proliferation of local task forces and the recent development of a national coalition. Federal, state, and local governments and private foundations have funded publicity campaigns, task forces, research studies, training programs, and other materials and service programs on elder mistreatment.

These strides are significant, considering that one of the first researchers in the field, Howard Segars, from the Legal Research and Services for the Elderly, in Boston, Massachusetts, stated that before that agency's research survey was developed, he was uncertain that domestic violence against the elderly was more than an occasional happening. This was because, even in the mid-seventies, there was no research to document its occurrence.

Yet research, program development, professional training, and coalition development is still in its infancy. Funding for programs is still quite scarce. There are few books and articles written on elder mistreatment assessment and intervention, and there has been no national research on the subject to help inform policy and program developers.

The following comprises the authors' suggestions on the future directions needed in elder mistreatment research, programming, and training.

RESEARCH

There is a vital need to formulate specific hypotheses and then to construct studies that test them with the employment of control groups. Another major need is to develop a uniform definition, so comparisons among studies can be made, allowing researchers to build on previous work. However, even if definitions do vary from study to study, each research effort should clearly elaborate the definition employed. Also, careful attention must be given to the selection of the sample group to avoid skewing, for example, by a particular client population or a particular agency. Pillemer (1986a) emphasizes the need to interview victims and perpetrators, as these perspectives may be especially instructive and differ substantially from case reports.

The following issues related to family mistreatment against the elderly require further research to better understand both the preventive and the interventive approaches to elder mistreatment:

(1) epidemiologic work to see if initial research results hold nationwide or if there are regional differences
(2) risk factors associated with mistreatment, including ageism
(3) prevalence of all forms of elder mistreatment
(4) the most sensitive signs and symptoms of the various forms of elder mistreatment
(5) similarities and differences between victim and perpetrator characteristics with each form of mistreatment
(6) effectiveness of mandatory reporting legislation
(7) effect of deinstitutionalization as an etiologic factor in elder abuse and neglect
(8) training models effective in fostering increased professional involvement in cases of elder mistreatment
(9) analysis of interventions for elder mistreatment victims that reduce the incidence and severity of abuse and neglect and those that do not
(10) testing the validity of the abuser categories outlined in Chapter 4

TRAINING AND PROGRAM DEVELOPMENT

Professionals working with the elderly need specialized training in the detection, assessment, and intervention of elder mistreatment in order to best help the victims and their families. Colleges and professional schools need to introduce curriculum on elder mistreatment so that their graduates will have a basic awareness upon graduation. This curriculum could be added to those existing for domestic violence and gerontology courses, if separate classes are not feasible.

Additional training materials need to be developed, such as films on intervention, training curricula on detection, assessment, and intervention, and training exercises.

There has been significant debate as to whether specialized programs for elder mistreatment victims need to be developed or whether existing social service and health care organizations can adequately provide for these victims. The authors recommend that each community should have, at the minimum, an elder mistreatment specialist available to help professionals working on difficult cases. This person could also conduct trainings for professionals, and possibly for volunteers, and help with referrals.

Organizations also need to develop and adapt site-specific protocols for their staff to help guide professional practice with this victim population. Several protocols for hospitals have already been developed, including the one from Harborview Medical Center in Seattle, which is in Appendix A of this book. The National Coalition of the Prevention of Elder Abuse, currently headquartered at the University of Massachusetts's Center on Aging, hopes to make these protocols, as well as other materials, available for those interested.

In some communities, organizations have been able to raise money to develop comprehensive service programs for elder mistreatment victims. But most localities are dependent on individual agencies developing services, without additional funding, that victims and their families require, for example, a caregiver support group. Only a handful of localities have developed a support group for victims, a service particularly useful in decreasing victim isolation and increasing self-acceptance. Also, agencies currently working with a special population, for example, battered women or drug abusers, need to consider ways of including older mistreatment victims or their abusers in their services. It is important that victims in every state have access to a 24-hour emergency hot line to receive support, advice, and basic information on elder mistreatment. And there are a paucity of services for those victims with one or more disabilities, especially emergency housing. Similarly, few localities have educational groups for batterers, and most of these are for men who abuse their wives. More of these programs need to be developed and expanded to include those who abuse nonspouse relatives and for female abusers.

Increasing the use of volunteers is a good way to add to the corps of people able to work with victims. These volunteers might be students, older people, people seeking to enter or reenter the work force, or those professionals interested in working pro bono. Volunteers are currently utilized in several elder mistreatment programs, and do a variety of activities, including public speaking, telephone reassurance calling with victims, accompanying victims to court, and other appointments provoking anxiety, and coleading support groups.

APPENDIX A
Elder Abuse and Neglect:
Written Protocol for Identification
and Assessment

"Tools" Needed

    (1) sketch sheet or trauma graph
    (2) tape measure
    (3) camera, film, flash
    (4) paper and pen
    (5) consent and release of information forms

General Interview Techniques (Villamore & Bergman, 1981)

    (1) privacy
    (2) pacing
    (3) planning
    (4) pitch
    (5) punctuality

ASSESSMENT

HISTORY

Methodology Technique

    (1) Examine client alone without caregiver.
    (2) Explain to caregiver he or she will be interviewed separately after client is inteviewed; this is part of routine exam.
    (3) Do not rush during interview. Provide support to client and caregiver. Work questions into conversation in relaxed manner.

(4) Do not be judgmental or allow personal feelings to interfere with providing optimal care. Do not *prematurely* diagnose client as a victim of elder abuse or neglect; do not tell caregiver what treatment plans are until facts are gathered.

(5) Pay special attention to trauma, burns, nutrition, recent change in condition, and financial status.

(6) Do collateral contacts as soon as possible with others, that is, visiting nurse, neighbors, friends, to obtain additional information.

PRESENTATION

Signs and Symptoms Suspicious for Abuse/Neglect

(1) Client brought in to hospital emergency room by someone other than caregiver.

(2) Prolonged interval between trauma/illness and presentation for medical care (i.e., gross decubiti).

(3) Suspicious history: client is new to system with history of "shopping" or "doctor hopping." Description of how injury occurred is alien to the physical findings, either better or worse; client has injuries not mentioned in history; has history of previous similar episodes; too many "explained" injuries or inconsistent explanations over time.

(4) Medication bottles or the client's pharmacy profile indicates medications are not being taken or given as prescribed.

Functional Assessment Evaluation

(1) Administer Mini-Mental State Exam or Dementia Scale to determine current mental status. (Kahn-Goldfarb Dementia Scale: 1 point each if patient knows age, day, month, year, month of birth, year of birth, street address, city, President of the United States, last past President of United States) (Poor = 0-2, Fair = 3-7, Good = 8-10).

(2) Collect pertinent data: i.e., length of time at residence, medical insurance source, income source(s).

(3) Assess client's ability to perform activities of daily living—i.e., ability to do self-care, ambulation status, ability to do meal preparation, pay bills, shop; model of transportation, etc.

(4) Ask client to describe a typical day to determine degree of independence or dependence on others, most frequent and significant contacts, who and how often seen.

(5) Ask client role expectations of self and caregiver.

(6) Have client report recent crisis in family life.

(7) Ask if there is alcohol use, drug use, mental illness, or behavior dyscontrol among household or family members.

(8) Ask directly if patient has experienced:

   (a) being shoved, shaken, or hit (record verbatim; when, where on body, examine body)

   (b) being left alone, tied to chair or bed, or left locked in room (record verbatim; when and duration)

    (c) having money or property taken or signed over to someone else. Determine current assets, financial status (specify)

    (d) withholding of food or medication or medical care, being oversedated with medication or alcohol

    (e) being threatened or experiences fear of caregiver

(9) Assess how client responds in situations listed above.

(10) Ask client how he/she copes with stress and upsetting incidents.

(11) Assess degree of patient's dependence on caregiver alone for financial, physical, and/or emotional support.

Physical Exam

(1) In medical setting, a standard comprehensive examination should be completed on a gowned undressed patient (no exceptions). In home, attempt review of body while protecting client's modesty.

(2) If injury is due to an accident, document circumstances (i.e., client was pushed, client has balance problem, patient was drowsy from medications and fell).

(3) Examine closely for effects of undermedication, overmedication, assess nutrition, hygiene, and personal care for evidence of abuse/neglect (i.e., dehydration or malnourishment without illness-related cause).

(4) Assess for

    (a) burns, unusual location or type

    (b) physical or thermal injury on head, scalp, or face

    (c) bruises and hematomas:

        (1) bilaterally on soft parts of body, not over bony prominences (knees and elbows), *inner* arm/thigh bruises are *very* suspicious

        (2) clustered as from repeated striking

        (3) shape similar to an object or thumb/finger prints

        (4) presence of old and new bruises at the same time as from repeated injury, injuries in different stages of resolution

Dating of Bruises

0-2 days	swollen, tender
0-5 days	red-blue
5-7 days	green
7-10 days	yellow
10-14 days	brown
2-4 weeks	clear

        (5) presence of bruises after changing health care provider or after prolonged absence from health care agency

    (d) mental status and neurological exam changes from previous level

    (e) fractures, falls, or evidence of physical restraint. Contractures may indicate confinement for long periods.

    (f) ambulation status: poor ambulation may be suggestive of sexual assault or other "hidden" injuries

(5) Observe and Document

    (a) size, color, shape, and location of injury. Use sketch sheet and/or take photographs.

    (b) no new lesions during patient's hospitalization

    (c) Family/caregiver(s) do not visit or show concern

    (d) client's affect and nonverbal behavior: abnormal/suspicious behavior or client—extremely fearful or agitated, overly quiet and passive, or expressing fear of caregiver

    (e) your intuition that all is not well between patient and caregiver

    (f) client—caregiver interaction: if the caregiver yells at client yells back, determine if they "need" to yell at each other and/or if this is a long-term pattern with which both are comfortable. On the contrary, if the verbal threats or yelling incidents are "new" behaviors and the contents of the yelling indicate escalation toward more abusive acts or severe verbal abuse, the practitioner should be concerned

(6) In medical setting, diagnostic procedures as indicated by history or exam may include:

    (a) radiological screening for fractures or evidence of physical restraint

    (b) metabolic screening for nutritional, electrolyte, or endorcrine abnormality

    (c) toxicology screening or drug levels for over- or undermedication

    (d) hematology screening for coagulation defect when abnormal bleeding or bruising is documented

    (e) CAT scan for major change in neurological status or head trauma that could result in subdural hematoma

    (f) gynecological procedures to rule out VD from sexual assault

INTERVIEW WITH CAREGIVER

Thank you for waiting while I interviewed your mother. Now it's your turn. I need your help—I am doing an (psychosocial) assessment of your mother's current functioning and situation in order to determine what services are appropriate at this time. I would like to spend some time with you and have you tell me your perception how things are here.

    (1) "Tell me what you want me to know about your mother."

    (2) "What is her medical condition? What medicine does she take?"

    (3) "What kind of care does she require?"

    (4) "How involved are you with your mother's everyday activities and care?"

    (5) "What do you expect her to do for herself?"

    (6) "What does she expect you to do for her?

        (a) And do you do those things?

        (b) Are you able to do them?

        (c) Have you had any difficulties? What kind?"

    (7) "Please describe how you spend a typical day."

    (8) "How do you cope with having to care for your mother all the time?"

    (9) "Do you have supports or respite care? Who and what? Are there other siblings who help?"

    (10) "What responsibilities do you have outside the home? Do you work? What are your hours? What do you do?"

(11) "Would you mind telling me what your income is?" (If this question seems touchy to the caregiver, say, "I just wondered if your family can afford the pills she needs to take." At the same time you are assessing the caregiver's degree of dependence on the elderly client's income/pensions/assets.)

(12) "Is your mother's social security check directly deposited in the bank?"

(13) "Who owns this house? Do you pay rent? Whose name is on the deed?"

(14) "If you help your mother pay her bills, how do you do it? Is your name on her account? Do you have power of attorney? Does it have a durable clause? When did you get it?"

Save More Delicate Questions for Last

(1) "You know those bruises on your mother's arms (head, nose, etc.). How do you suppose she got them?" (Document response verbatim. If possible, follow up with request that caregiver demonstrate how injury may have happened.)

(2) "Your mother is suffering from malnourishment and/or dehydration," or, "Your mother seems rather undernourished and thin; how do you think she got this way?"

(3) "Is there any reason you waited this long to seek medical care for your mother?"

(4) "Caring for someone as impaired as your mother is, is a difficult task. Have you ever felt so frustrated with her that you pushed her a little harder than you expected? How about hitting or slapping her? What were the circumstances?" (Record verbatim.)

(5) "Have you ever had to tie your mother to a bed or chair, or lock her in a room when you go out at night?"

(6) "Have there been times when you've yelled at her or threatened her verbally?"

Signs of High-Risk Situation

(1) Alcohol use, drug abuse, and/or mental illness in caregiver's residence.

(2) Cargiver is alienated, socially isolated, has poor self-image.

(3) Caregiver is young, immature, and behavior indicates own dependency needs have not been met.

(4) Caregiver is forced by circumstances to care for patient who is unwanted.

(5) Caregiver is unemployed, without sufficient funds, dependent on client for housing and money.

(6) Caregiver's and/or client's poor health or chronic illness may exacerbate poor relationship.

(7) Caregiver exhibits abnormal behavior, for example, overly hostile or frustrated, secretive, shows little concern, demonstrates poor self-control, "blames" client, exhibits exaggerated defensiveness and denial, lacks physical contact, lacks facial or eye contact with client, shows overconcern regarding correcting client's bad behavior, visits patient with alcohol on breath.

COLLATERAL CONTACTS

(1) Do collateral contacts promptly before caregiver attempts to collude with patient.

(2) Number of contacts may range from 2 to 17.

DIAGNOSIS

Integrate patient history, physical exam, caregiver history, and collateral contact information.

- (1) No evidence for elder abuse/neglect
- (2) Suspicion of neglect
- (3) Suspicion of abuse
- (4) Positive for abuse/neglect, gross neglect

TYPES OF CLIENTS (Villamore & Bergman, 1981)

- (1) Competent, consenting
- (2) Competent, nonconsenting
- (3) Incompetent
- (4) Emergency

INTERVENTION OPTIONS

AGENCY/PROFESSIONAL INTERVENTION

Indirect Intervention

- (1) Documentation—review of chart may later point to abuse.
- (2) Reporting—most states have Adult Protective Services Units. Approximately 40 states have some form of reporting law, some are mandatory reporting laws, some are voluntary reporting laws.
- (3) Referral out—refer the case to another agency for follow-up.

Direct Intervention to Client

- (1) Diagnostic plan
    - (a) Geriatric evaluation team home visit or in-clinic assessment
    - (b) Short hospital stay or repeated contact for further assessment and case planning
    - (c) Administer written protocol and refer case for execution of treatment plan
- (2) Therapeutic plan
    - (a) Repeated home visits or appointments in office to gain trust, to persuade and bargain with elderly client, to help elder with decision making, ventilation, problem solving (takes up to two years)
    - (b) Legal intervention—use least restrictive option to the extent possible (see scale of legal interventions), that is apply for guardianship or protective payee status; press charges and/or prosecute
    - (c) Financial crisis intervention:
        - (1) call the bank to place an alert on the account.

(2) transport the client to the bank to discuss the incident with the bank manager
(3) bring bank personnel to the client's home
(4) report the incident(s) to the social security office
(5) attempt to void the client's signature on forms signed without the client's knowledge or recall, on forms signed under duress, or when the client most likely was legally incompetent

(3) Education plan/empowerment training to acquire/strengthen positive, powerful self-image.
    (a) assertiveness training
    (b) how to fend off an attacker
    (c) how to care better for self to reduce dependency on caregiver
    (d) advise elder not to have observable pattern of behavior (i.e., change walking route regularly when going to and from store, bank, etc.)

(4) Environmental change—use the least restrictive environmental option to the extent possible (see range of interventions).
    (a) block watch
    (b) move to safer place, that is elderly housing, another friend, relative, adult foster home, boarding home
    (c) home improvements
    (d) increased contacts outside of home, that is day-care center

(5) Advocacy resource linkage
    (a) assist elder with obtaining meals-on-wheels, chorework service
    (b) link elder to natural helpers and "gatekeepers"
    (c) telephone checks, that is Dial-A-Care

Direct Intervention to Caregiver

(1) Therapeutic Plan
    (a) repeated home or office visits for family counseling to clarify role expectations and reduce conflict
    (b) respite care for elder to give caregiver a rest
    (c) obtain cash grants for caregiver when possible

(2) Educational Plan
    (a) group programs—community-wide information meetings and small informal discussion of groups. Provide information on aging resources and aging process, mutual problem solving and support. Help improve ability to cope with elder and to recognize own needs and limitations.
    (b) individual contacts, articles to explain "normal" dependency of aging, "senility," Alzheimer's disease, and so forth

(3) Resource linkage
    (a) strengthen resources and social supports available to caregivers, i.e., chorework, home health aide

STAFF TRAINING

(1) Teach your colleagues how to detect abuse/neglect, what intervention options are, what is being done elsewhere.

(2) Offer team approach to caring of high-risk patients/clients; offer to do follow-up, share information.

COMMUNITY INTERVENTION

a. Utility Worker
b. Postal Worker
c. Waiter/Waitress
d. Apt. Manager
e. Grocery Clerks

1. Gatekeepers

Agency ←→ Case ←→ Natural   2. Neighbors
Resources   Managers   Helpers
                                 3. Relatives

(1) Train "gatekeepers" to watch for symptoms of elderly's inability to care for self, for abuse and neglect, and to report to case manager when an elder has not been seen for a long time.
(2) Maintain regular contacts in your geographical area with the natural helpers and institution staff, that is bank personnel.
(3) Always engage the natural helper's or elderly's own social systems in carrying out the treatment plan. If possible, do not "rescue."

FOLLOW-UP PROCESS

(1) In general, make appointments for initial home and in-agency visits.
(2) Consider dropping in on client for second visit to put all involved "on warning" but also to display earnestness.

LIMITATIONS/WHEN TO TERMINATE

(1) The client dies.
(2) The client is competent and chooses not to accept the practitioner's help.
(3) The client is no longer in danger.

From "Detection and Treatment of Elderly Abuse and Neglect: A Protocol for Health Care Professionals," S. Tomita, *Physical Therapy and Occupational Therapy in Geriatrics* 2, (2), Haworth Press, Inc., New York. Copyright © 1982. Reprinted by permission.

APPENDIX B
Dementia Scale

(1) What is the name of this place?
(2) Where is it located (address)?
(3) What is today's date?
(4) What is the month now?
(5) What is the year?
(6) How old are you?
(7) When were you born (month)?
(8) When were you born (year)?
(9) Who is the president of the United States?
(10) Who was the president before him?

Poor = 0-2
Fair = 3-7
Good = 8-10

From R. L. Kahn et al., *American Journal of Psychiatry* 117, pp. 326-328, 1960. Copyright © 1960, the American Psychiatric Association. Reprinted by permission.

APPENDIX C
Mini-Mental Status Exam

ORIENTATION

Ask each of the following, and score 1 for each correct answer.

(1) What is the day of the week   , month   , date   , year   ,
season   ( )/5

(2) Where are we: state   , county   , town   , residence number   ,
street name   (or hospital and floor)   ( )/5

REGISTRATION

Name 3 unrelated objects slowly and clearly (i.e., horse, watch, phone).

Ask the client to repeat them. Tell client to remember objects because
he/she will be asked to name them in a few minutes. Score first try.
Repeat objects till all are learned, up to 6 trials.   ( )/3

ATTENTION AND CALCULATION

Ask the client to perform serial 7 subtraction from 100 or serial 3 subtraction from 20. Stop after 5 numbers and score 1 for each number
(93, 86, 79, 72, 65) or (17, 14, 11, 8, 5).   ( )/5

RECALL

Ask the client to recall the names of the 3 unrelated objects which you
asked him/her to repeat above and score 1 for each correct name.   ( )/3

LANGUAGE

(1) Naming—point to 2 objects and ask client to name them. Score 1
for each correct name (e.g., tie and pencil).   ( )/2

(2) Repetition—ask the client to repeat "No ifs, ands, or buts." Allow
only 1 trial. Score 0 or 1.   ( )/1

(3) Three-stage command—ask the client to "Take a paper in your
right hand, fold it in half and put it on the floor." Score 1 for each
part correctly executed.   ( )/3

(4) Reading—print on a blank card "close your eyes," ask the client to
read the sentence and do what it says. Score 1 if eyes are closed.   ( )/1

(5) Writing—ask the client to write a sentence; do not dictate. It must
contain a subject and verb, and make sense. Correct grammar and
punctuation are not necessary. Score 0 or 1.   ( )/1

(6) Copying—ask the client to copy this figure
exactly. All 10 angles and intersection
must be present to score 1.      ( )/1

Total ( )/30 possible points

(Refer to source for scoring guidelines)

REFERENCES

Alliance/Elder Abuse Project (1983). An analysis of states mandatory reporting laws on elder abuse. (unpublished, Syracuse, N.Y.).

Block, M. R. & Sinnott, J. D. (1979). The battered elder syndrome: An exploratory study. (unpublished, University of Maryland).

Butler, R. N. (1969). Ageism: Another form of bigotry. *The Gerontologist 9*, 243-246.

Ellis, A. (1973). *Humanistic psychotherapy*. New York, McGraw-Hill.

Finkelhor, D. (1983). Common features of family abuse. In D. Finkelhor et al. (Eds.), *The dark side of families: Current family violence research*. Beverly Hills, CA: Sage.

Finkelhor, D. & Pillemer, K. (1984). "Elder abuse: Its relationship to other forms of domestic violence. Presented at the Second National Conference on Family Violence Research, Durham, N.H., August.

Folstein, M. F., Folstein, S. E., & McHugh, P. R. (1975). Mini-mental state. *Journal of Psychiatric Research 12*(3), 189-198.

Fulmer, T. & Ashley, J. (1986). Neglect: What part of abuse? *Pride Institute Journal of Long Term Home Health Care 5*(4), 18-24.

Gelles, R. (1974). Child abuse as psychopathology: A sociological critique and reformation. In S. Steinmetz & M. Straus (Eds.), *Violence in the family*. New York: Dodd-Mead.

Greene, M. G., Adelman, R., Charon, R., & Hoffman, S. (1986). Ageism in the medical encounter: An exploratory study of the doctor-elderly patient relationship. *Language and Communication 6*, 113-124.

Hwalek, M., Sengstock, M. & Lawrence, R. (1984). Assessing the probability of abuse of the elderly. Presented at the Annual Meeting of the Gerontological Society of America, San Antonio, TX.

Johnson, T. (1986). Critical issues in the definition of elder mistreatment. In K. A. Pillemer et al. (Eds.), *Elder abuse: Conflict in the family*. Dover: Auburn House.

Kahn, R. L., Goldfarb, A., Pollack, M., & Peck, A. (1960). Objective measures for the determination of mental status in the aged. *American Journal of Psychiatry 117*(4), 326-328.

Legal Research and Services for the Elderly (1981). In *Elder and abuse and neglect: A guide for practitioners and policy makers*. San Francisco: National Paralegal Institute and Author.

National Paralegal Institute and Legal Research and Services for the elderly (1981). In *Elder abuse and neglect: A guide for practitioners and policy makers*. San Francisco: Author.

Ne, I. F. (1979). Choice, exchange and the family. In W. R. Burrett et al. (Eds.), *Contemporary theories about the family*. New York: Free Press.

O'Malley, T. A. (1986). Abuse and neglect of the elderly: The wrong issue? *Pride Institute Journal of Long Term Home Health Care 5*(4), 25-28.

Phillips, L. R. (1983). Abuse and neglect of the frail elderly at home: An exploration of theoretical relationships. *Journal of Advanced Nursing 3*, 379-392.

Pillemer, K. A. (1986a). Risk factors in elder abuse: Results from a case-control study. In K. A. Pillemer et al. (Eds.), *Elder abuse: Conflict in the family*. Dover: Auburn House.

Pillemer, K. A. (1986b). The hidden sorrow: An overview. Tape 1 of film series *Elder Abuse and Neglect in the Family*. University of Massachusetts Medical Center, University Center on Aging, Massachusetts.

Pillemer, K. A. & Finkelhor, D. (1986). The prevalence of elder abuse: A random sample survey. Presented at the Gerontological Society of America Meeting (November).

Pillemer, K. A. & Finkelfor, D. (1988). The prevalence of elder abuse: A random sample survey. *The Gerontological Society of America 28*(1), 51-57.

Quinn, M. J. & Tomita, S. (1986). *Elder abuse and neglect*. New York: Springer.

Salend, E., Kane, R., Satz, M., & Pynoos, J. (1984). Elder abuse reporting: Limitations of statutes. *Gerontologist 24*(10), 61-69.

Steinmetz, S. & Anderson, D. (1983). Dependency, family stress and abuse. In T. Brubaker (Ed.), *Family relationships in later life*. Beverly Hills: Sage.

Strauss, M. A., Gelles, R., & Steinmetz, S. K. (1980). *Behind closed doors: Violence in the family*. Garden City, NY: Anchor/Doubleday.

Tomita, S. (1982). Detection and treatment of elderly abuse and neglect: A protocol for health care professionals. *Physical Therapy and Occupational Therapy in Geriatrics 2*(2), 37-51.

Walen, S. R., DiGiuseppe, R., & Wessler, R. L. (1980). In *A practitioners guide to rational-emotive therapy*. New York: Oxford University Press.

Watts, D. & McCally, M. (1984). Demographic Perspectives. In C. K. Cassel et al. (Eds.), *Geriatric Medicine: Principles and Practice*. NY: Springer-Verlag.

Wolf, R., Godkin, M., & Pillemer, K. A. (1984). *Elder abuse and neglect: Report from the model projects*. Worcester, MA: University of Massachusetts Medical Center, University Center on Aging.

Wolf, R. S. (1986). Major findings from three model projects on elderly abuse. In K. A. Pillemer et al. (Eds.), *Elder abuse: Conflict in the family*. Dover: Auburn House.

Wolf, R. S. & Pillemer, K. (in press). *Helping elderly victims: Findings from three model projects on elder abuse*. New York: Columbia University Press.

Zuckerman, C. & Dubler, N. (1986). *Discharge planning for elderly patients of diminished capacity*. New York: Montefiore Medical Center.

ABOUT THE AUTHORS

RONALD D. ADELMAN, M.D., is a graduate of the Albert Einstein College of Medicine. His involvement in geriatric education has been extensive. His contributions to the growth of geriatrics have included work in areas of health promotion and disease prevention, patient-physician interaction in the medical encounter, and methods by which the geriatric focus can be integrated in all four years of medical education. While he was an Assistant Professor in Clinical Medicine at Columbia University at Presbyterian Hospital, he helped to design a required segment on the geriatric patient for medical students and was actively involved in house staff teaching. For several years he has held the title of Adjunct Assistant Professor of Sociology at Hofstra University, where he has taught courses on such topics as Death and Dying and Contemporary Medicine. After leaving Columbia, he came to the Mt. Sinai Medical Center, Ritter Department of Geriatrics and Adult Development. Initially, he was deeply involved in directing the medical student clerkship in geriatrics, and later he became the Director of the Fellowship Program in Geriatrics. He also developed a Well Elderly Program in conjuction with the 92nd Street Y on the Upper East Side of Manhattan. This program exposes medical students to the concepts of health promotion and disease prevention as applied to older adults as well as combat negative stereotypic attitudes medical students may have concerning the geriatric patient and aging in general. He has also served as physician administrator for the Mt. Sinai/Victim Services Agency Elder Abuse Project, which is focused on training Mt. Sinai health providers in detecting, assessing, and intervening in elder mistreatment cases. He recently became Chief of the Division of Geriatrics at Winthrop University Hospital, a major affiliate of Stony Brook Medical School. He remains on faculty at the Ritter Department of Geriatrics at Mt. Sinai Medical Center.

RISA S. BRECKMAN, M. S. W., received a B.A. in Women's Studies and Psychology from Antioch College and a Masters in Social Work from Adelphi University. She holds a Primary Training Course Certificate in Rational-Emotive Theory and Techniques from the Institute for Rational-Emotive Therapy. She has worked with crime victims for over 10 years. In the mid-seventies she worked at a shelter for battered women in Oregon, one of the first in the country. She received rape crisis counseling training from the St. Vincent's Hospital's Rape Crisis Center in New York City and volunteered with that program for over five years. She was Senior Planner with the Victim Services Agency in New York City, developing programs for rape victims, victims with disabilities, child abuse victims, and elder abuse victims. She developed and directed the nationally recognized Elder Abuse Project, sponsored by the Victim Services Agency, which provides individual, family, and support group services for elder abuse victims, recruits, and trains senior volunteers to work with the victims, and provides training and case consultations to professionals working with elder abuse victims. Currently, she is the Co-director of the Elder Abuse Training and Resource Center, which provides training, technical assistance, and case consultation services to organizations in the United States and Canada. To date, she has trained thousands of professionals in elder abuse detection, assessment, and intervention. She is also currently a clinical consultant to the Mt. Sinai/Victim Services Agency Elder Abuse Project. Her work has been featured in many newspapers, magazines, and on radio programs, including *The New York Times* and *Parade* magazine.